Chas. T. Rothermel

Portraits and Biographies of the Fire Underwriters of the City of Chicago

Chas. T. Rothermel

Portraits and Biographies of the Fire Underwriters of the City of Chicago

ISBN/EAN: 9783744690003

Printed in Europe, USA, Canada, Australia, Japan

Cover: Foto ©ninafisch / pixelio.de

More available books at **www.hansebooks.com**

PORTRAITS AND BIOGRAPHIES

OF THE

Fire Underwriters

OF THE

CITY OF CHICAGO

COMPILED AND PUBLISHED BY

CHAS. T. ROTHERMEL & CO.,
234-236 LA SALLE STREET.
CHICAGO.

DECEMBER, 1895

Press of
Monarch Printing and
Binding Company,
Chicago.

A GREAT many people have, during the last twenty-five years, noticed and inquired the meaning of a handsome gold badge or watch charm which is worn by a few of the older Underwriters, a cut of which is shown above. This charm is not only beautiful in its design and execution, but it has a history which is interesting as well.

Soon after the Great Fire occurred in this city on October 9 and 10, 1871, the Fire Insurance Adjusters began to look about for a headquarters where they could meet, compare notes, and confer about the hundreds of losses which required adjustment, and, in most of which they each had an interest. Rooms 6, 7 and 8, on the second floor of what was then known as the Sherman House, on West Madison Street (now the Gault House) were selected, and for months afterwards frequent meetings were held and claimants by the hundred were interviewed, their claims adjusted and paid. It was a sort of a clearing house, and the adjusters organized a club and jointly employed clerks, stenographers, appraisers, notaries, etc.

It appears that during the busy days of the work of adjusting, Mr. W. F. Storey, then the owner, editor and proprietor of *The Times*, called to see about his loss, and finding a large crowd of people waiting for a similar purpose he became impatient, and repairing to his sanctum, he dashed off a sensational editorial about the "delay," "red tape," etc., in getting a loss adjusted. He had probably been told that he would have to await his turn, as he complained about the delay; however that may be, he closed his double leaded editorial by stating that there ought to be inscribed over the door of No. 6 Sherman House, the words, "Who enters here leaves hope behind;" and that the skull and cross-bones would also be appropriate. Whether he also made use of the well-known Latin quotation, **"soc et tu um"** is not now remembered; at any rate, the adjusters caught the idea of having a little gold souvenir badge made and presented to each member, which was carried out, and these badges are now highly prized by those of their owners who are still living, one of whom kindly loaned us his, from which the above drawing was made.

(3)

Officers,

Managers,

General Agents

and Assistants.

CHARLES E. AFFELD,

Of the Firm of Witkowsky & Affeld, General Agents.

Charles E. Affeld was born at Stettin, Prussia, on the 10th of March, 1843. His parents came to this country in 1847, arriving in Chicago by steamer from Buffalo, in October of that year, with three children, two boys and one girl. The two boys, Charles E., and Frank O. (the latter now U. S. Manager of the Hamburg-Bremen Insurance Co.), are twins, and attended the Dearborn School at Chicago until 1859, and completed their education at Bryant & Stratton's Business College.

When the war broke out in 1861, Mr. Affeld and his brother enlisted at the first call for troops, in Battery B., 1st Illinois Artillery, or "Taylor's Battery," and served three years with distinction, most of the time under Generals Grant and Sherman, in the Fifteenth Corps. He was mustered out in July, 1864, and in the fall of that year accepted a clerkship in the Recruiting Department of the Provost Marshal's office in this city. He was engaged in the subscription book business in 1865, and in 1868 commenced his Insurance career as a Broker, and after the Chicago fire of 1871, took the position of Surveyor for the N. Y. Underwriters' Agency, then in the hands of Ogden, Sheldon & Scudder, and afterwards with James B. Floyd. In 1873 he formed a partnership with Conrad Witkowsky as General Agents for the H. B. Fire Insurance Company, of Hamburg, Germany, which Company they have represented with success for the last twenty-three years, at the same time representing other companies as Local Agents.

Mr. Affeld was married July 5th, 1868, to Miss Helen Waite, of Chicago, and has four children living.

He has been a member of the Chicago Board of Trade since 1873; is a member of the Union League Club; Germania Manner-Chor; North Shore Club; Chicago Board of Underwriters; Northwestern Underwriters' Association; Academy of Science; and Thomas Post No. 5, G. A. R., of this city.

(7)

BENJAMIN AUERBACH,

Of the Firm of Pellet & Hunter, General Agents.

Benjamin Auerbach was born at Chicago in 1859 and was educated in the schools of that city. He started in the Fire Insurance business shortly after the fire in 1871, with a firm of brokers, and has since been identified with the general and local business, with the exception of three years which were spent in mercantile business. He has been connected with the present firm for about eleven years.

Mr. Auerbach is a member of several Chicago clubs.

CHARLES HART BARRY,

Associate Manager of the Western Department of the Pennsylvania Fire
Insurance Company.

Charles Hart Barry was born at Alton, Illinois, November 15th, 1857, and is a son of the late Amasa S. Barry, a prominent adjuster of fire losses. Mr Barry was a graduate of the University of Illinois in 1877, and entered the Fire Insurance business in a Local Agency at Alton. Two years later found him in the Chicago office of the Niagara Fire. In 1881 he was appointed Special Agent of the Phœnix of London, for Illinois, Indiana, Ohio and Michigan, and in 1884 State Agent and Adjuster for the Insurance Company of North America and Pennsylvania Fire for Southern Illinois, and afterwards for Michigan. In 1890 he became a member of the firm of J. F. Downing & Co., of Erie, Pa., Western Managers of the two last named companies. When the Pennsylvania Fire decided, in 1894, to establish a Western Department of its own, Mr. Barry was appointed Manager, in conjunction with Mr. John H. Davis.

Mr. Barry was married at Alton, Illinois, to Miss Ida M. Bateman and has one child. He is a member of the Knight Templar Belvidere, No. 2, Alton, Illinois; the Union League Club, of Chicago, and the County Club of Evanston.

J. S. BELDEN,

Manager, London & Lancashire Insurance Company of Liverpool, England.

John Secord Belden was born at Warsaw, New York, September 8th, 1839. He was educated in the Public Schools of that place and at the Warsaw Academy. He came to Chicago in 1862, and began his connection with the Insurance business in 1865 as Accountant with the Security Insurance Company, in which office he remained until 1871, and with the German-American until 1888. He was appointed Manager of the London and Lancashire in 1888, having charge of fourteen Western States and three Territories.

Mr. Belden was married December 17th, 1868, to Miss Amanda W. Pool, and has four children, three sons and one daughter. He is a member of the Union League Club, and of the Kenwood Club, of Chicago.

I. S. BLACKWELDER,

Manager, Niagara Fire Insurance Company of New York.

I. S. Blackwelder was born on a farm near Litchfield, Montgomery County, Illinois, on the 8th day of March, 1840. His father was one of the pioneers of Illinois, settling in Montgomery County in 1833, and his grandfather was a soldier in the Revolutionary War, enlisting from North Carolina.

He received his education in the common schools and the Academy at Hillsboro, Ill. and in 1861 was elected County Clerk of Montgomery County, which position he held until 1865, when he engaged in the mercantile business. Two years later he accepted an appointment as Special Agent for the Ætna Insurance Company, and for thirteen years held a similar position for various companies, including the Franklin, Imperial, Scottish Commercial and Lancashire, excepting two years of that time—1874 to 1876—when he was in the service of the National Board of Fire Underwriters as its Supervising Agent for the Western States. In April, 1881, Mr. Blackwelder took charge of the Western Department of the Niagara Fire Insurance Company of New York.

Mr. Blackwelder was married April 5th, 1877, at Lawrence, Kas., to Miss Alice Gertrude Boughton. They have two children, both boys.

He is a member of the Union League Club, Sons of the American Revolution and Masonic Lodge.

(11)

CHARLES EDWARD BLIVEN.

Charles Edward Bliven was born at Phelps, Ontario County, N. Y., September 21st, 1835. When he was six years of age his family removed to Toledo, Ohio, where he entered the public schools. His business career began in 1848, when he was employed as a messenger in the first telegraph office opened at Toledo. He was advanced to an operator's desk and later was appointed Superintendent of important railroad telegraph lines, which position he resigned to enter the Ohio Wesleyan College. In 1861 he enlisted in the Union army and served in the military telegraph department. In 1863 he was appointed Captain on the staff of General M. C. Meigs in the Army of the Potomac and was stationed at Cincinnati, in the Quartermaster's Department. He was mustered out with the rank of Major in 1866. During the war Major Bliven had opportunities for studying law at the Cincinnati Law School and on leaving the army he was admitted to the Ohio Bar and practiced several years at Toledo, later becoming interested in a local insurance agency, and afterwards being appointed State Agent for Ohio of the Manhattan Insurance Company of New York. He was the organizer and secretary of the first Ohio State Board of Underwriters, and also one of the promoters of the Fire Underwriters' Association of the Northwest, serving as its first secretary, which position he held from 1871 to 1876, and as president in 1877. In 1871 Major Bliven accepted the Western General Agency of the Howard Insurance Company, of New York, which position he held until 1885, when he entered upon the duties as General Manager of the Western Department of the American Fire Insurance Company of Philadelphia, which office he resigned on May 1st, 1895, on account of ill-health. Major Bliven is a 33d degree Mason, a prominent member of the Loyal Legion and other fraternal and social organizations and has always taken an active interest in the public matters of the Western Metropolis.

GEORGE WILLIAMS BLOSSOM.

Assistant General Agent National Fire Insurance Company.

George Williams Blossom was born at Dubuque, Iowa, on the 1st of October, 1854. He received his education in Dubuque, attending the public schools and the high school. After leaving school he engaged in the Book and Stationery business for a few months, and in 1870 entered the Local Insurance office of Smith & Plaister, at Dubuque. In 1873 he came to Chicago and entered the office of the German-American Insurance Company, under Eugene Cary, advancing from Supply Clerk to Chief Examiner, until in 1884 he assisted in organizing the Western Department of the Connecticut Fire Insurance Company, under A. Williams, remaining there until 1887, when he became a partner in the firm of Fred S. James & Co., and also Assistant General Agent of the Washington Fire and Marine Insurance Company, which later re-insured in the National Fire Insurance Company, of Hartford, Conn.

Mr. Blossom is a member of the Union League, Kenwood, Hyde Park and Kenwood Country Clubs. He was married in Chicago to Miss Carrie R. Boardman and has two children, both boys.

WILLIAM C. BOORN,

Assistant Manager of the London and Lancashire Insurance Company of England.

William C. Boorn was born at Kenosha, Wisconsin, August 30th, 1863, his ancestors having lived in America for many generations. He was educated in the public schools at Peoria, Illinois, and engaged in the Insurance business in August, 1881, in the Chicago office of the Orient Insurance Company. He remained in the Orient office until the present office of the London and Lancashire was opened in 1888 under Manager Belden, and has occupied the position of Assistant Manager and taken general charge of the office ever since.

Mr. Boorn is a member of the Union League, Carleton and Mendelssohn Clubs of Chicago.

MORELL O. BROWN,

General Agent. Westchester Fire Insurance Company of New York.

Morell O. Brown was born in Clarence, New York, July 10th, 1847. When a boy his parents moved to Springfield, Ohio, and in 1861 to Terre Haute, Indiana.

In 1864, Mr. Brown enlisted in the 133rd Indiana Regiment, serving with credit. After the close of the war he was employed by the Postoffice Department in the Railway Postal work. His Insurance career began in 1868, as Solicitor and Clerk in a Local Agency at Terre Haute, Ind. In 1869 he removed to Indianapolis as bookkeeper in a Local Agency, becoming a partner in the following year. Later he was employed as Special Agent for several companies, and on October 22d, 1871, just after the great Chicago fire, entered the service of the Westchester Fire Insurance Company of New York, and has continued with the company ever since as its General Agent for the Western Department; he is also a director in the company.

Mr. Brown is a genial gentleman of fine social qualities, a popular member of the Union League and Illinois Clubs, and recognized among the Insurance fraternity as an accomplished Underwriter.

THOMAS JEFFERSON BROWNE,

Secretary and Manager, Garden City Mutual Fire Insurance Company
of Chicago.

Thomas Jefferson Browne was born in Seneca County, Ohio, April 11th, 1849. He received his primary education in the common schools and then took a three years' course in the Scientific Department of Heidleberg University, of Tiflin, Ohio, after which he taught school for a time in six different states. Later he was admitted to the bar and practiced law at Ottawa, Illinois, and at Fowler, Indiana. In 1873 he entered the Insurance business at Tiflin, Ohio, and in 1875 was employed by P. G. Gardner as fieldman, and later by Adolph Loeb & Co., as Special, resigning to engage with H. H. Walker in the same capacity, in Indiana, for the Home Insurance Company of New York, and later was Special with other companies. He has been continuously in the Insurance business since 1874, and has been very successful in his underwriting.

Mr. Browne was married October 25th, 1874, to Miss Suthie A. McCully of Ottawa, Illinois, He is a member of the Oddfellows and also of the Masonic order.

(16)

HENRY W. BUSH,

Assistant Manager of the Fire Association of Philadelphia.

Henry W. Bush was born at Kalamazoo, Michigan, November 29th, 1847, receiving his education in the common schools of Jackson, Michigan.

He commenced his business life in a country store, in Jackson, entering the Insurance business in 1866 at the same place.

In 1875 he came to Chicago and engaged with W. H. Cunningham, having been previously engaged with him in field work. In 1892 he was appointed to his present position, Assistant Manager of the Fire Association of Philadelphia.

Mr. Bush was married to Miss Hanna P. Frisbie, at Chicago, in October, 1869.

EUGENE CARY.

Eugene Cary was born in Boston, Erie County, New York, February 20th, 1835. His early years were spent in hard work on the farm. When sixteen years old he started out for himself. He taught school several terms; then studied law, first at Sheboygan, Wis., with Judge David Taylor, late of the Wisconsin Supreme Court; afterwards at Buffalo with Judge James Sheldon and Judge Nathan K. Hall. In 1856 he began the practice of his profession at Sheboygan, Wis., was soon after elected City Attorney, and the next year, when twenty-two years old, was made County Judge of Sheboygan County, at that time one of the most populous and wealthy counties in the State.

When the War of the Rebellion came in 1861, he was prompt to enlist in his country's service and served during the war, first as Captain in the First Wisconsin Volunteer Infantry, and subsequently as Judge Advocate on the staff of the General commanding the First Division of the Fourteenth Army Corps (Army of the Cumberland). After the war he settled in Nashville, Tenn., and served one term in the State Senate and one term as Judge of the Circuit Court. He began his insurance experience in 1857, as Local Agent for the Aetna and Hartford Insurance Companies at Sheboygan. After the war he served for a time as State Agent for the Aetna in Tennessee. In October, 1871, he came to Chicago for the Imperial Insurance Company, organized and was Manager of its Western Department until 1873, when he accepted the management of the Western Department of the German-American Insurance Company, which position he has held ever since.

Judge Cary, as an Underwriter, while progressive, is at the same time cautious and conservative. He despises pretense and clap-trap; prefers profitable results rather than large figures, and the success of the company under his charge has given ample testimony of the wisdom and efficiency of his methods.

He was for two terms President of the "Union" and has always taken an active part in its counsels.

Judge Cary takes special pride in the patriotic record of his family. Himself a soldier of the Union, he had two brothers in the Union army, both surgeons, one of whom died in the service. One of his uncles was a soldier in the American army in the War of 1812, and was killed in battle. His grandfather was a Revolutionary soldier, and his ancestry back to the arrival of the first of them, more than two hundred and fifty years ago, at Plymouth colony, always bore an honorable and loyal part in their country's service and history.

In the spring of 1883 Judge Cary was a candidate for Mayor of Chicago on the Republican ticket, the nomination having been entirely unsolicited. Although he failed to get the office, it is now generally conceded that he received a majority of the legal votes cast, but was defeated by the peculiar counting out methods then in vogue.

No company has achieved better results in the West than the German-American, and none is more successful to-day.

EUGENE CARY,
Manager, German-American Insurance Company of New York.

THOMAS SEPTIMUS CHARD,

General Manager of the Fireman's Fund Insurance Company of California.

Thomas Septimus Chard is the son of English parents and was born in Buffalo, New York, April 15th, 1844. He attended the common schools of Buffalo and subsequently studied three years at Clarence Classical Academy. He received his early business training in his brother's bank at Buffalo, and in 1864 arrived in Chicago and entered the employ of F. A. Howe in the Transportation business. In 1868 Mr. Chard became a correspondent in the office of the Lumberman's Insurance Company, of Chicago, of which company his uncle, Thomas Goodman, was president. In January, 1870, he entered the employ of the Fireman's Fund Insurance Company, as Special Agent for the West, and was appointed Manager July 1st, 1872, and has probably done the longest service for one company of any of the Chicago managers. He was Organizing Secretary of the Union and for two years its President.

Mr. Chard was married to Miss Adeline Peabody Whitney in 1877, and is one of the prominent members of the Union League Club.

(20)

JOHN WILLIAM GUNNISON COFRAN,

Assistant General Agent of the Western Department of the Hartford Fire Insurance Company.

J. W. G. Cofran was born at Goshen, N. H., in 1855. He spent his boyhood on a farm and obtained his education in the district school and at Kimball's Union Academy, at Meriden, N. H. When he was nineteen years of age he removed to San Francisco and entered the employ of the Commercial Insurance Company of California as an office boy. So well did he apply himself to the business that five years later he was appointed Special Agent of the Commercial for Oregon, Washington and Idaho, with headquarters at Portland. In 1881 the Hartford management, noting the ability of the young man, appointed him its Special Agent for the same territory. After five years service as joint special for the Commercial and Hartford, Mr. Cofran was called back to San Francisco to take the position of Associate Manager of the Hartford for the Pacific Department, his colleague being Henry K. Belden. He remained in this position until his recent appointment as Assistant General Agent of the Company for its Western Department. Mr. Cofran has served as Vice-president and Chairman of the Executive Committee of the Fire Underwriters of the Pacific. He is a member of the Pacific Union, Olympic and Merchants' Clubs, of San Francisco; also of the Chamber of Commerce and Merchants' Exchange. Though a young man, Mr. Cofran has served the Hartford for a good many years, and came to Chicago with a reputation of being a well-equipped and progressive Underwriter, well fitted for his work.

(21)

ALVA C. COLLINS,

Secretary of the Firemen's Insurance Company of Chicago.

Alva C. Collins was born at Burlington, Ky., May 18th, 1860, and was educated in Union Christian College at Merom, Indiana. He is the son of a minister and was moved about over the country in very early life. For some years after leaving college he taught school and in 1881 entered the Insurance business at Danville, Illinois. From 1885 to '88 he was in the Life Insurance Business, was Secretary of the Northwestern of Huron, and later State Agent for Kentucky, Indiana, and West Virginia for the National Life and Maturity Insurance Company of Washington, D. C.

Mr. Collins was married at Paris, Illinois, September 9th, 1886, to Miss Caroline F. Church, and has two children.

SYDNEY TENISON COLLINS,

Assistant Manager, Central Department of the Fireman's Fund Insurance Company of California.

Sydney Tenison Collins was born in Ireland, November 19th, 1857, and is consequently 38 years of age.

With a desire to see something of the world, he crossed the Ocean in 1872, landing at Quebec, Canada. Finding his way from thence to Montreal, he entered the service of the head office for Canada of the Phœnix Assurance Company of London, as policy clerk, remaining with that company until 1879. In that year, Mr. C. F. Mullins, then Manager of the Western Department of the Commercial Union, learning of Mr. Collins through an acquaintance in Montreal, made him a proposition to come to Chicago, and August, 1879, saw Mr. Collins located at 162 LaSalle Street, occupying an important position in the Commercial Union office. His advancement was rapid, until he became Chief Clerk in that office, from which position he retired to accept the Western Management of the Anglo-Nevada Assurance Corporation, in 1888, afterwards succeeding to the management of its successor, the "Caledonian," first at Chicago and afterwards at Philadelphia. The consolidation of the Caledonian and Niagara resulted in Mr. Collins withdrawing from the first-named company and returning to Chicago in February, 1893. At the opening of the fair, Mr. Collins was appointed Assistant Secretary of the Insurance Auxiliary Committee of the World's Columbian Exposition, and during the Fair had charge of the Insurance interests at Jackson Park. At the close of the Fair on November 1st, 1893, the Assistant Managership of the Fireman's Fund was offered him, and in that capacity he serves to-day.

Mr. Collins resides at Hinsdale, Illinois, is married and has three children.

Mr. Collins' eldest brother, Edward Tenison Collins, B. L., is resident Secretary for Ireland, at Dublin, of the North British and Mercantile Insurance Company.

JAMES C. CORBET,

Assistant Manager, Lancashire Insurance Company.

James C. Corbet was born in New York City, June 19th, 1855. He was educated in the public schools of New York, and when 16 years of age, entered the Insurance Agency of Edward Haslehurst. He began his labors the day following the Chicago fire, and remained with the agency eight years. For four years, commencing with 1880, he was out of the Insurance business, serving during that time as bookkeeper for the American News Company. His tastes, however, were in the direction of Insurance, and in November, 1884, he entered the employ of the Lancashire Insurance Company as a clerk in the New England Department. A year later he was appointed chief examiner of that department, and in 1887, New England Special Agent of the company, with headquarters in Boston. He held this position until January 1st, 1892, when he was called to the New York office, and appointed Assistant Secretary of the General American Department. In July, 1893, Mr. Corbet was appointed Deputy Assistant United States Manager, and six months later was transferred to Chicago as Assistant Manager of the Western Department.

(21)

GEORGE D. CORLISS.

Assistant Manager, Western Department of the Merchants' Insurance Company of Newark, N. J.

George D. Corliss was born at Cincinnati, Ohio, August 19th, 1865, and was educated at the Chickering Institute of that city, his parents being natives of New Hampshire.

Mr. Corliss entered the office of the Western Department of the Germania Fire Insurance Company of New York in 1887, serving there in various capacities for something over seven years. He was appointed Chief Clerk and Examiner in the Merchants, of Newark, Western Department, December 1st, 1894, and received the appointment of Assistant Manager, July 1st, 1895. He is by nature and education one of the conservatives in the business.

CHARLES DURAND COX,

Of the Firm of Cox & Meeker.

Charles Durand Cox was born at Lyons, Iowa, April 27th, 1863. He was educated in the public schools of Rock Island, Ill., and took a business course in Bryant & Stratton's Business College at Davenport, Iowa.

He has had ten years' experience in office and field work with Western Mutuals, and for the last five years has been manager of the Western Department of Underwriters at American Lloyds, New York, now holding the same position for this and eleven other fire insurance institutions, whose business is confined to the insuring of protected properties.

He was married on the 8th of November, 1888, and has one daughter.

Mr. Cox is a member of the Union League Club and Chicago Athletic Club, Knights Templar, Oriental Consistory, Mystic Shrine and is a 32d degree Mason.

WILLIAM H. CUNNINGHAM,

Manager of the Fire Association of Philadelphia, Pa.

William H. Cunningham was born at Harrisburg, Penn., November 6th, 1838, and was educated in the Common Schools with one term at Harrisburg Academy. He moved to Dubuque, Iowa, and in April, 1859, entered the Insurance business, with Mr. Allison, then a Local Agent, representing the Unity of London, Continental of New York, Security of New York, Phenix of Brooklyn, and others. He came to Chicago in June, 1862, and was the first Clerk employed by J. R. Payson, who at that time established the Western Department of the Security Insurance Company of New York. In 1864 he was made Assistant General Agent, and in 1867 succeeded to the Western Management of the Company. The Company succumbed to the large losses caused by the great Chicago Fire of October, 1871. In 1872 he was made General Agent of the Fire Association and American Fire Insurance Company, both of Philadelphia, the latter withdrawing its department in 1884, the Fire Association continuing up to the present time.

Mr. Cunningham is a member of the Union League and Kenwood Clubs of Chicago.

(27)

R. S. CRITCHELL.

Robert S. Critchell was born at Glastonbury, England, January 18th, 1844. When he was two years old his family came to the United States, settling at Rochester, N. Y. In 1855 the family moved to Cincinnati, Ohio. While a school boy he was seized with the ambition to earn his own living and become a successful business man, and very much against the desires of his parents, he secured a position as office boy in the Insurance Agency of Samuel E. Mack & Co., which was at the time (1857) a prominent agency in Cincinnati, representing such companies as the Home, Continental and other companies.

In 1860, Mr. Mack, the head of this firm was appointed Western General Agent of the Home, at St. Louis. Mr. Mack was so much attached to the subject of this sketch that he induced him to go to St. Louis with the new enterprise. Here he remained for two years, when he returned to Cincinnati and became a clerk in the Western Department of the Ætna Insurance Company of Hartford, then in charge of J. B. Bennett.

In 1863 he went into the United States navy (Mississippi squadron) as a junior officer, and was in the service until the close of the war, when he returned to St. Louis and was at once appointed Special Agent for the Home Insurance Company, and until 1868 traveled throughout the Western and Southern States as Special Agent of that company. In 1868 he came to Chicago as Special Agent of the Phœnix Insurance Company of Brooklyn, in which capacity he had supervision of the business of that company for eight states, having as assistants in his territory some gentlemen who have since become very prominent in the business, such as Mr. A. J. Harding of the Springfield F. & M. Insurance Company, Judge Ostrander of the Phœnix of Brooklyn, and others.

In 1870 he added to his business the Chicago Agency of the Phœnix of Brooklyn and other companies, and at the time of the great fire, in 1871, his Local Agency was the first after the fire to open an office, the first to pay a loss, and the first to issue a policy.

At the present time, in addition to being Manager of the Western Departments of the Insurance Company, State of Pennsylvania, and the Teutonia of New Orleans, Mr. Critchell is Manager of the Cook County Department of the Caledonian Insurance Company of Scotland and the Spring Garden Insurance Company of Philadelphia, and is head of the firm of R. S. Critchell & Co., which, in point of the number of sole agencies represented and premiums written for the companies represented, is the largest in the City of Chicago.

Mr. Critchell is a strong believer of the Sole Agency plan, his convictions being that the Local Agents in large cities, whose business is sufficient to occupy their whole time, and who have been trained to the business, should be as responsible for the results of the business as anyone connected with the companies. The twenty-five years' experience in which the premiums of R. S. Critchell & Co.'s Agency run largely into the millions, with losses under 45 per cent, he claims, justifies his position.

In Chicago he has been prominent in commercial and social circles, having been for six years connected with the Union League Club as Vice-president, Secretary and Director. For a number of years after the second large fire (in 1874) he was an active member on various committees of Citizens' Association and Board of Underwriters, which secured important reforms in the City of Chicago, the results of whose actions have made underwriting successful in Chicago since. He is now a member of the Union League Club, Kenwood Club, Treasurer of the Illinois Commandery, Naval Order of the United States, member of the Congregational Club, and Director in the Western State Bank.

He was married in 1866 at St. Louis to Miss M. A. Mooley, daughter of Judge Mooley, of that city, and has four children, one of which, Robert M., is a partner in his business. His home, on Greenwood avenue, is an ornament to that part of the city, and his principal source of pleasure.

R. S. CRITCHELL,

Manager Insurance Company of the State of Pennsylvania and the Teutonia
Insurance Company of New Orleans.

(29)

ALEXANDER H. DARROW,

General Agent. Western Department of the Agricultural Insurance Company of Watertown, N. Y.

Alexander H. Darrow was born at Clarendon, Orleans County, New York, November Michigan. In August, 1862, he enlisted and was assigned to Company M of General Sheridan's old regiment, the Second Michigan Cavalry, and served until the close of the war. For the first year and a half he was almost constantly engaged in field duty; the balance of his military life was as military bookkeeper in Gen. Grant's office. In 1868 he came to Chicago and soon after entered the employ of the Republic Insurance Company. Beginning as a clerk he was promoted to the position of cashier of the Company, which was the only Chicago Company that paid in full the losses sustained by the great fire. In 1872 he became the State Agent of the Agricultural Insurance Company of Watertown, New York, with which corporation he has ever since been identified.

In November, 1866, Mr. Darrow was married to Miss Susan C. Johnston, daughter of William Johnston, of Marshall, Michigan, an early settler of that place.

Mr. Darrow is a member of the Illinois Club, the Masonic Fraternity and Columbian Post, Grand Army of the Republic. He supports the Republican party, though never an active politician.

(30)

JOHN H. DAVIS,

Associate Manager, Western Department of the Pennsylvania Fire Insurance Company.

John H. Davis was born in the City of Philadelphia, August 17th, 1844. He was educated in his native city and in Massachusetts, and for several years prior to entering the Insurance business served as a Reporter on the "Philadelphia Press." On May 1st, 1867, he began his work as a Fire Insurance Underwriter in the City of Albany, N. Y., with the New York State Department of the Liverpool and London and Globe Insurance Company, then in charge of James Hendrick as General Agent, with whom he remained for five years, after which he returned to Philadelphia, and for nearly ten years thereafter was actively engaged in field work in the Eastern, Middle and Western States, for the Union of Philadelphia, and other Eastern Companies. In September, 1881, Mr. Davis took charge of the Mechanics' Insurance Company of Philadelphia, as Secretary, and after seven years of successful management he resigned and was elected General Agent at the Home Office of the Pennsylvania Fire, where he remained until appointed one of the Western Managers of the Company at Chicago, on January 1st, 1895.

A. F. DEAN,

Assistant Manager, Springfield F. & M. Insurance Company of Springfield,
Mass.

EDWARD FRANK DeFOREST,

General Western Agent of the Farmer's Fire Insurance Company of York, Pennsylvania.

Edward Frank DeForest was born in New Haven, Conn., on the 20th of July, 1846, being of French descent. He received his education principally in the schools of New Haven, and is a graduate of Yale Law School. After leaving college he practiced law in New Haven for a year, and then came West and opened a law office in Decatur, Illinois. In 1870 he went to St. Louis, Mo., and entered the general office of the North Missouri Insurance Company, remaining there until the fall of 1874, when he came to Chicago, and after a few months' traveling as Special Agent, settled at Rockford, Illinois, and opened a local agency. In 1882 he was appointed Assistant Secretary of the Cedar Rapids Insurance Company of Cedar Rapids, Iowa, and in February, 1883, left that position for the one he now holds with the Farmer's of York.

Mr. DeForest was married at Madison, Wis., September 8th, 1884, to Miss Alma L. Peirce, who died March 25th, 1895, leaving no children. He is a member of the Century Club of Elgin, Illinois, where he makes his home.

(33)

DAVID T. DEVIN,

Manager, Western Department of the Reliance Insurance Company of Philadelphia, and the Delaware Fire Insurance Company of Philadelphia.

David T. Devin was born in Sangamon County, Illinois, on the 6th of September, 1849. He took a Civil Engineering course at Cornell University, New York. He was first engaged as a Civil Engineer and Railway employee, and entered the Insurance business as clerk in a Local Agency office at Des Moines, Iowa. From May 15th, 1882, to February 1st, 1893, he was Special Agent for the Glens Falls Insurance Company of New York. On the 1st of February, 1893, he became Manager of the Western Department of the Delaware Insurance Company and the Reliance Insurance Company of Philadelphia.

On the 26th of October, 1875, Mr. Devin was married to Miss Ida Shane, daughter of Judge John Shane, of Vinton, Iowa. He is a member of the Chicago Athletic Association.

M. F. DRISCOLL,

General Agent, Phoenix Assurance Company of London.

(35)

WALTER W. DUDLEY,

United States Manager of the Manchester Fire Assurance Company of England.

Walter W. Dudley was born at Guilford, Conn., in the year 1845. He began his education in the public schools of Connecticut, and removing to Wisconsin at an early age, continued it in the schools of that State. He entered the Insurance business as a Farm Solicitor, then went into a Local Agency office at La Crosse, Wis., first as clerk, then as partner. Resigning from this position he went to St. Paul, Minn., and became connected with the St. Paul Fire and Marine Insurance Company, afterwards traveling for the same company as Special Agent over a wide territory. He remained with this company four years, after which he became connected with the German-American as Special Agent. At the end of eight years' service with this company he resigned and engaged in Banking business at Jamestown, North Dakota. While there he was offered a position with the Western Department of the North British and Mercantile Insurance Company, as Assistant Superintendent, which position he accepted and held for five years, the last two of which he was Superintendent of the Western Department. His next position was with the Manchester Assurance Company, with which he is still connected.

Mr. Dudley was married at Pottstown, Penn., in 1880, to Miss Elizabeth M. Beecher. They have one daughter. He is a member of the Union League Club of Chicago.

CHARLES D. DUNLOP,

Manager, Providence Washington Insurance Company of Rhode Island.

Charles D. Dunlop was born at Lexington, Missouri, on the 18th day of January, 1863. He received his early education in the Common Schools, subsequently taking a course in the Pennsylvania University of Mining, and after leaving College was engaged for some time in mining. He became connected with the Insurance business at Denver, Colo., in 1883, with the firm of Cobb, Wilson & Co., and later was appointed Manager of the Providence Washington Insurance Company at that place. In 1895, Mr. Dunlop was transferred to Chicago, assuming charge of the Western and Mountain Departments of the Company.

In 1891, Mr. Dunlop was married to Miss Rosemary Conwell at Cincinnati, Ohio.

HENRY CLAY EDDY,

Resident Secretary, Commercial Union Assurance Company, Limited, of England.

Henry Clay Eddy was born at Providence, Rhode Island, on the 9th of May, 1848, received his education in the grammar schools and took a course in a military academy. When a boy he entered the Providence, R. I., agency of the Home Insurance Company of New York, and early in 1867 went to the main office of the company, resigning to establish an agency in Philadelphia, in September, 1871. In 1874 he went to the New York office of the German-American, and from 1876 to 1881 was Special Agent for said company in New England, with headquarters at Boston. Transferred to a similar position with the Phenix of Brooklyn, where he remained until 1883, when he went to the Commercial Union in New York and eventually came to Chicago in 1884. Was President of the Fire Underwriters' Association of the Northwest in 1891.

Mr. Eddy was married December 26th, 1869, at Brooklyn, N. Y., to Miss May Eldridge, and has four children. He is a member of the Union League and Washington Park Clubs, and the Masonic Lodge.

TRUMAN W. EUSTIS,

Assistant General Agent of the Western Department of the Phenix of Brooklyn.

Truman W. Eustis was born at Port Washington, Wis., October 25th, 1857. At the early age of eleven he lost his father and had his own way to make in the world. The family removed to Chicago, and here the education of young Truman was received in the Grammar and High Schools. At the age of seventeen he began active life as an office boy with the local agency of the Phenix. Here he did such good work that he was transferred to the General Agency Department, being advanced until he became daily report examiner. In October, 1884, he was appointed Special Agent and Adjuster for several Southern States, including Kentucky and Tennessee. After two years of this special work he was called back to Chicago as General Adjuster of the department. In this capacity he continued until January, 1891, with eminent success, when he was appointed Supervisor and Adjuster for sixteen of the principal cities in the West and South, contributing much to the growth of the company in the entire field. Upon the death of Mr. Thos. Burch, the General Agent of the department, in June, 1892, and the appointment soon after of Eugene Harbeck as his successor, Mr. Eustis was promoted to the position of Assistant General Agent, and with the ability which has, during his underwriting career been characteristic of his work, he has continued in that position ever since.

(39)

GEORGE MARSHALL FISHER,

Manager, Western Department of the Palatine Insurance Company of Manchester, England.

George Marshall Fisher was born at Painesville, Ohio, on the 15th of November, 1857. He was educated in the Common Schools of Painesville; was graduated from the High School in 1876, and then attended the Western Reserve College at Hudson, Ohio. From January 1st, 1880, he was three years in the Local business at Painesville, Ohio, and was then appointed Special Agent of the Insurance Company of North America, and Pennsylvania Fire Insurance Company, in Ohio and West Virginia, which position he retained until 1885, when he accepted the position of General Correspondent in J. F. Downing's General Agency office at Erie, Pa. After a year there he became Special Agent for the same Companies in Indiana and Ohio, and September, 1887, was appointed Special Agent of the London Assurance Corporation for Michigan, Indiana, Kentucky and Tennessee, under the management of Chas. L. Case. He served in that position until September 1st, 1892, when he was appointed Manager of the United Fire Re-Insurance Company, and the Palatine Insurance Company, Ltd., of Manchester, England, for the Western Department (which is independent, reporting direct to the home office at Manchester, England), with jurisdiction over fourteen States—Ohio, Indiana, Michigan, Illinois, Wisconsin, Minnesota, N. Dakota, S. Dakota, Iowa, Nebraska, Kansas, Missouri, Kentucky and Tennessee.

Mr. Fisher is a member of the Union League and Chicago Athletic Clubs, and the Delta Kappa Epsilon College Society.

SAMUEL EUGENE FORSYTHE,

Manager, Globe Fire Insurance Company of New York.

Samuel Eugene Forsythe was born at Cape Vincent, New York, April 9th, 1849. He attended Academy at Fulton, New York, for some years, and later was graduated from the Law Department of the Albany University, Albany, New York. He first engaged in Mercantile pursuits and entered the Insurance business at Watertown, N. Y., in 1872, and with the exception of six years has been constantly engaged in field work, having acted in the capacity of Special Agent throughout New England, the Middle, most of the Western and some of the Southern States.

EDWARD E. FOSTER,

Assistant Manager, Western Department of the Germania Fire Insurance
Company of New York.

(42)

BYRON WHITNEY FRENCH,

General Agent of the Orient Insurance Company.

Byron Whitney French was born in Ontario County, in New York State, October 17th, 1837, and received his education in the Common Schools of that State. He began his business career in 1853 as clerk in an Insurance office, which position he resigned to enter the drug business, continuing in the same from 1854 to 1859, when he returned to the Insurance business and later became Local Agent, remaining as such until 1867, when he was appointed Special Agent, which position he held until 1873, when he accepted the position he now holds as General Agent of the Orient Insurance Company.

Mr. French was married at Dansville, N. Y., October 22d, 1862, to Miss Martha Brown. Has four sons and one daughter.

CHARLES BROWN FRENCH,

Assistant Manager, Manchester Fire Assurance Company.

Charles Brown French was born in 1863 in New York. At an early age he came to Chicago, and was educated in the public schools of that city, afterward graduating at Amherst College. In 1879 he entered the Fire Insurance business in a Local agency office in Chicago. Subsequently he became connected with the Orient Insurance Company and served that Company as Special Agent in various fields. In 1888 he was appointed Assistant General Agent, but resigned that office two years later to take his present position with the Manchester Fire Assurance Company.

Mr. French was born, bred and brought up in the insurance business. To him it is largely a matter of heredity as he is the third generation of his family to engage in the business in Chicago. He was married at Hamilton, Missouri, in 1895 to Miss Pearl Ellen Ross, and is a member of the University and Apollo Clubs of Chicago.

S. S. FROWE,

Assistant Secretary, Commercial Union Assurance Company of London.

S. S. Frowe enlisted in the Eighteenth Wisconsin Infantry October 16th, 1861, and, serving through the war, rendered conspicuous services on important details and staff duty, and at its close held a Captain's commission. In 1866 he entered the Insurance business and has been continuously a member of the profession, occupying places of high responsibility and trust. In 1868 he went to the Aetna as a Special Agent in Iowa; in 1871 he cast his lot with the Andes in the head office at Cincinnati, being one of the Chief Examiners. Subsequently, during Mr. J. B. Bennett's management of the Western Department of the Continental, he was Special Agent for that company. In April, 1881, he was appointed by the Commercial Union Assurance Company, Limited, of London, one of its Special Agents and assigned to duty in Illinois; a year later he was made its General Adjuster at the Western Department, serving in that capacity until July, 1888, when he was appointed Assistant Secretary at the Western Department and is still discharging the duties of that position.

RUDOLPH H. GARRIGUE,

Manager, Western Department, The Merchants' Insurance Company of Newark, New Jersey.

Rudolph H. Garrigue was born in Brooklyn, New York, February 19th, 1857; was educated in Common Schools and Packard's Business College of New York City, and has been engaged in Fire Insurance all his business life, which he entered as office boy in the office of the New York Underwriters' Agency on the 36th of August, 1873. He was moved along under gradual promotions, through various office positions, and was appointed Special Agent of the New York Underwriters' Agency in January, 1877, as Assistant to Geo. D. Gould, in Illinois, Iowa and Nebraska. Was transferred to Indiana and Michigan, October 1st, 1879, and made State Agent for Michigan, February 19th, 1881, which position he resigned September 4th, 1883, to take charge of organizing the Western Department of the Germania Fire Insurance Company, with title of Assistant Manager. He resigned from the Germania August 30th, 1894, on completion of twenty-one years' service, and in December of the same year he was appointed Manager of the Western Department of The Merchants' Insurance Company of Newark, New Jersey, which position he still holds.

Mr. Garrigue's grandfather sold his farm where the Chicago Court House now stands for $700 and thought he had a good thing, in 1836. His father organized and built up the Germania Fire Insurance Company from 1858 to 1891, starting the Company with $200,000 gross assets, which had grown to over three millions when he died, as President.

Mr. Garrigue was married at Kendallville, Indiana, February 19th, 1881, to Miss Lida M. Collier, the daughter of Capt. Merwin F. Collier, who was for twenty years Indiana State Agent of the New York Underwriters' Agency. He is a member of the Masonic Fraternity.

CHARLES B. GILBERT,

Manager of the Lancashire Insurance Company of England.

Charles B. Gilbert was born at Watertown, New York, on the 24th of October, 1854, and was educated in the Public Schools of that place. His first business experience was in the line of Insurance in the office of the St. Paul Fire & Marine Insurance Company, in St. Paul, Minn., in 1868; he was for several years Secretary of said Company, and after various experiences incidental to the life of an Insurance man we now find him in the position of Manager of the Lancashire Insurance Company.

Mr. Gilbert was married in Milwaukee, Wisconsin, to Miss Alice Mabbett and has three children, two girls and one boy. He is a member of the Union League and Kenwood Clubs of Chicago besides several clubs in St. Paul.

(47)

WARREN F. GOODWIN.

Of the Firm of Goodwin, Hall & Henshaw, Fire Underwriters.

Warren F. Goodwin was born at Boston, Mass., in 1857. He graduated from the Brooklyn Polytechnic Institute in 1873, and at once engaged in the Fire Insurance business, entering the New York office of the London Assurance Corporation, then managed by Frame, Hare & Lockwood. He remained there until October, 1882, when Henry H. Hall, United States Manager of the Northern of London, offered him a position in the Agency Department of that Company, which he accepted. January 1st, 1887, he was appointed Manager of the Central Department of the Northern, with headquarters at Cincinnati. His territory included the States of Ohio, Indiana, West Virginia, Kentucky, Tennessee and Arkansas. This position he retained until July 1st, 1893, when the Central and Northwestern Departments of the Northern were consolidated into one Western Department with headquarters at Chicago. Mr. Goodwin and Mr. W. D. Crooke were appointed Associate Managers. In May, 1894, Mr. Goodwin resigned his position with the Northern Assurance Company, to form, in connection with Messrs. Hall and Henshaw of New York, the firm of Goodwin, Hall & Henshaw, Mr. Goodwin taking personal charge of the business at Chicago. This firm was at once appointed Managers of the Western Department of the Union Assurance Society of London, and General Agents for the West of the Citizens' Insurance Company of New York, and the Virginia Fire and Marine Insurance Company of Richmond.

In addition to their General Agency business they conduct a Local Agency, representing the Union Assurance Society of London, the Grand Rapids Fire Insurance Company of Grand Rapids, the Virginia Fire and Marine Insurance Company of Richmond, the German Insurance Company of Peoria, the Commercial Insurance Company of Cincinnati, the Commercial Union Assurance Company of London and the Norwood Insurance Company of New York. They also do a large brokerage business.

HOWARD PINKNEY GRAY,

Vice-President and General Agent, Hanover Fire Insurance Company
of New York.

Howard Pinkney Gray was born at Baltimore, Maryland, December 17th, 1840, of Scotch parents, and was educated in public and private schools of Baltimore. He commenced business as clerk in a store, and then as an engineer in the United States Navy. Entered the Insurance business in 1876, at Mobile, Alabama. In 1877 entered the service of New York Underwriters' Agency, and remained with them seventeen years.

Mr. Gray was married October 5th, 1869, to Miss Imogene Skinner, of Oswego, New York, and has three children. He is a member of the Evanston Lodge, Chapter and Commandery, Oriental Consistory, Medinah Temple of Chicago, Columbia Post, G. A. R., and Farragut Naval Veteran Association.

J. C. GRIFFITHS,

Associate Manager, North British and Mercantile Insurance Co.

J. C. Griffiths was born at Gloucester, England, in 1843, and emigrated to this country at the age of fifteen. He was in Cairo, Illinois, during the war, part of the time in the naval department under Commodore Porter, and removed to Chicago in 1868. That year he commenced his successful Insurance career with the then Republic Fire of Chicago, continuing with that company until the memorable disaster of 1871. Then he became Cashier and Bookkeeper in the local and general agency department of the Home of New York, in Chicago, and in 1880 he was appointed state agent of that company for Wisconsin. This position he occupied to its increasing satisfaction for eleven years, until December 31st, 1890, when he resigned to accept the resident secretaryship of the North British and Mercantile at Milwaukee for the State of Wisconsin and the Michigan Peninsula, in which field he has done successful work.

EDWARD G. HALLE,

Manager, Western Department of the Germania Insurance Company of
New York.

(51)

EUGENE HARBECK,

General Agent, Phenix Insurance Company of Brooklyn, N. Y.

Eugene Harbeck was born at Batavia, New York, in 1853, and came West in his boyhood, receiving his education in the Public Schools of Battle Creek, Michigan. In 1870 he entered the insurance business in a Local Office at Battle Creek, Mich., and has risen step by step, from Office Boy to Clerk, Solicitor, Agent, Special Agent, Adjuster, Secretary and General Agent. He was married at Battle Creek, March 13th, 1877, to Miss Emma Grey Wattles and has one son, now seventeen years old.

Mr. Harbeck is a Mason and a member of the Union League Club.

AMOS JOSEPH HARDING.

Manager, Western Department of the Springfield Fire and Marine Insurance
Company.

Amos Joseph Harding was born near Galion, Ohio, May 2d, 1839, of New England
ancestry and parentage, his direct ancestors having settled in Plymouth Colony in 1623.
His early years, up to the age of fourteen, were spent on a farm, during which time
he attended the District Schools of the neighborhood. His academical education was
obtained at Ohio Central College. Upon leaving college a brief period was spent in
teaching country schools, after which, when eighteen years of age, he emigrated to the
then new territory of Nebraska, and settled in Nebraska City. He was engaged for a
time as United States Deputy Surveyor of the public lands in the new territory, and
in January, 1858, commenced his Insurance career as surveying or sub-Agent of the
Aetna Insurance Company of Hartford. He continued in the local Insurance business, in
connection with other mercantile pursuits, until the breaking out of the war in 1861,
when he enlisted as a private in the First Nebraska Infantry, in which he served for two
years, when he was transferred by promotion to the Sixth Missouri Cavalry, with which
he continued, until mustered out, with the rank of Captain, in September, 1865. His
war service was wholly in the West, and mainly in the Thirteenth and Fifteenth Army
Corps in the Army and Department of the Tennessee, and in the Department of Missouri.
At the close of the war he returned to Nebraska, and re-established himself in the
Local Insurance business, and for many years represented at that point the Aetna, Hartford Fire of Hartford, Home Phenix and Continental Insurance Companies of New York,
and the Insurance Company of North America. In addition to his local business Mr.
Harding was for several years the Special Agent and Adjuster for the Home Insurance Company of New York, in Kansas and Nebraska. Immediately after the great
Chicago fire of 1871 he took charge, as supervising Special Agent and Adjuster of the
interests of the Phenix Insurance Company of New York, in the States of Missouri,
Iowa and Kansas, Nebraska and the Western territories. When the Springfield Fire
and Marine Insurance Company determined to organize a Western Department he was
called into its service, January 1st, 1876.

P. P. HEYWOOD,

General Agent of the Hartford Fire Insurance Company.

Mr. Heywood was born in Westminster, Mass., and spent his boyhood on a farm. He was educated in the public schools and Academy of his native town and at Lester Academy, Mass. He began at an early age to teach in the public schools of his State. He taught one year in Portsmouth, Va.

He came to Illinois, in 1855, locating at Aurora, where for nine years he had charge of the Public Schools of that city, laying the foundation thoroughly for a system of Public Schools which for years has given Aurora a leading position among the cities of the State and country. His health failing, he came to Chicago in January, 1864, and in September of that year entered the Insurance office of Moore & Stearns. Soon after he was made Secretary of a Local Company which reinsured its business in a few months by his advice. The next year, in January, 1866, he entered the office of G. F. Bissell, General Agent of the Hartford Fire Insurance Company, as Special Agent, traveling over the entire West. In July, 1869, he went into local business in Chicago for a year with Mr. C. H. Case. In November, 1869, he was made General Agent for the Hartford for its Pacific Department, and located at San Francisco, January 1st, 1870. He remained there until January, 1872, having located the Company in all the States and Territories of that field. At a later date he left that department in the hands of his associate, A. P. Flint, and returned to Chicago, entering the office of the Western Department of the Hartford as Assistant General Agent with G. F. Bissell, which position he held until July 1st, 1895, when he was promoted to the position of General Agent, owing to the death of G. F. Bissell.

Mr. Heywood was one of the first members of the Union League Club; was one of its Board of Managers for three years, and was Vice-President from 1891 to 1893. He is also a prominent member of the Marquette Club, Chicago Literary Society, Illinois Society of the Sons of the American Revolution, Massachusetts Society in Chicago, of which he was President last year.

His family consists of two sons: Henry B., Special Agent for the Hartford in Nebraska and South Dakota, and John P., who is engaged in the lumber business in this city.

(51)

ROCKWOOD WILDE HOSMER,

General Agent. Mercantile & American Insurance Company of Boston. Mass.

Rockwood Wilde Hosmer was born at Concord, Mass., in March, 1845, and is a graduate of the High School of that town. He commenced business as office boy in a wholesale dry goods house in Boston, connecting himself with Fire Insurance in 1862, as clerk in the office of I. F. Dodson & Co., in Boston, Mass., and has remained in the same business continuously up to the present time.

Mr. Hosmer is a member of the Chicago and Union Clubs, the Society of the Sons of the American Revolution, and for several years past has been President of the Chicago Board of Underwriters.

R. J. O. HUNTER,

Of the Firm of Pellet & Hunter, General and Local Agents.

R. J. O. Hunter was born in Hamilton, Canada, in 1852, and received his education at Toronto and New York, with the exception of four years spent in private schools in England and France. In 1871 he began the study of law at Cincinnati, Ohio, but subsequently moved to Chicago, where he completed his legal studies and was admitted to the bar by the Supreme Court at Springfield, Illinois. After several years' practice, however, on account of trouble with his eyes, he was compelled to give up active work in his profession, and moved to Kansas City, in 1879, where he became associated with Ed. H. Webster, in the Fire Insurance business, under the firm name of Webster & Hunter. In January, 1884, Mr. Hunter concluded to return to Chicago and formed a partnership with Oakley B. Pellet, under the firm name of Pellet & Hunter. In January, 1887, Oakley B. Pellet died and was succeeded by his son, Clarence S. Pellet, the firm name remaining unchanged. Mr. Hunter has been an active and earnest worker in the Chicago Fire Underwriters' Association, until within a few years, since when the growth of the firm's General Agency Department required him to give his entire attention to the outside business. The firm of Pellet & Hunter are General and Local Agents for the Mechanics' of Philadelphia, United States Fire of New York and the Manufacturers' and Merchants', Armenia and Citizens' Insurance Companies of Pittsburg.

JOSEPH W. HOSMER,

Of the Firm of R. W. Hosmer & Co., General Agents.

Joseph W. Hosmer was born in Concord, Massachusetts. His ancestors, who were prominent in early colonial days and during the Revolution, came from England in 1635 and settled in Concord, Mass. He was educated in the public schools of Concord, and commenced business in the Stove Factory of Pratt & Wentworth in Boston. He was admitted to a partnership interest in the firm and sent to Chicago in 1868 to take charge of the business there, which was continued until the great fire of 1871. In 1873 he became connected with the firm of R. W. Hosmer & Co., which connection has continued ever since.

Mr. Hosmer was married at Barre, Vermont, in 1879, to Miss Ella Fifield. He is Vice President of the Mechanics' Institute of Chicago, and a member of the Union League Club of Chicago and the Illinois Society of the Sons of the American Revolution.

FREDERICK SINCLAIR JAMES.

General Western Agent of the National Fire Insurance Company.

Frederick Sinclair James is a native of Illinois and was born at Barrington, Cook County, February 20th, 1849. His father was prominent in public affairs in Chicago and Cook County for many years, was Provost Marshal for the Western District during the war, and for a time Fire and Police Commissioner of Chicago. Mr. James received his education in the Public and High Schools of Chicago. On July 18th, 1864, he entered the Insurance office of Alfred James & Co., as office boy, the senior member of the firm being his brother. In four or five years he had worked his way up to a membership in the firm, and not long after the great Chicago fire began business on his own account as a Local Agent. Gradually, as the head of the firm of Fred S. James & Co., he has built up the largest Local Agency in Chicago, and has also for many years served as General Western Agent for strong Companies. For several years he was Western Manager of the Fire Insurance Association of London, England, and afterward of the Boston Underwriters' until the Washington Fire and Marine withdrew from the combination, when he continued as its General Western representative, and when the National of Hartford reinsured the Western business of the Washington, continued as its Western General Agent.

Mr. James is prominent in social circles, a member of several clubs and a thirty-second degree Mason, with a deserved popularity wherever known. He was married at Chicago, October 6th, 1868, to Miss Loretta B. Whitney and has five children.

O. C. KEMP,

General Agent, Rochester German Insurance Company of Rochester, N. Y.

JOSEPH A. KELSEY,

Assistant Manager, Western Department, Royal Insurance Company.

Joseph A. Kelsey was born at St. Mary's, Ohio, in 1858. He began his insurance career in 1880 in Denver, in the Local and General Agency of Cobb, McMann & Co. In 1881 he was appointed Special Agent of the New York Underwriters' Agency with head-quarters at St. Louis, and a year later he became associated with the General Agency of Martin Collins of that city. On the 1st of February, 1884, Mr. Kelsey was employed by Manager Downing of the Insurance Company of North America as Special Agent for Iowa with headquarters at Des Moines. After remaining in that State for two years he was transferred to Indiana as State Agent for the same company, which position he occupied until January, 1890. He was then offered and accepted the position of assistant to Mr. E. L. Allen, Manager of the Northwestern Department of the Royal at Chicago. With the consolidation of the Central and Northwestern Departments of this company August 1st, 1895, Mr. Kelsey was made assistant by the in-coming Managers, Messrs. Law Brothers. Mr. Kelsey comes of an Insurance family. His father, Benjamin Kelsey, has been State Agent of the Hartford in Indiana for the past twenty years. One of his brothers, H. N. Kelsey, is State Agent for Illinois and Indiana for the Norwich Union, and another brother, Preston T. Kelsey, is the Illinois State Agent for the Hanover.

Mr. Kelsey is a member of the Union League and Chicago Athletic Clubs.

GEORGE E. KLINE,

Assistant General Manager, Continental Insurance Company of New York.

George E. Kline was born at Lebanon, Penn., on the 16th of December, 1859, and obtained his education at Faribault, Minn. He entered the insurance business with the Continental Insurance Company at Chicago, November 24th, 1879.

GEORGE WALLACE LAW,

Associate Manager, Western Department of the Royal Insurance Company.

George Wallace Law was born in Cincinnati, Ohio, August 6th, 1852, not long after his father, Dr. John S. Law, removed from Georgia to Cincinnati. He received a liberal education, sufficient to prepare him for Yale, from which his father graduated with honors. Instead, however, of pursuing a full literary course, he entered the office of his father, the Manager of the Royal, and from clerical to field work, he made himself thoroughly familiar with all details of Fire Underwriting; later becoming associated with his brothers, John H. and Charles H., as one of the managers of the Central Department of the Royal, and now as one of the active managers of the Department, comprising fourteen States, with headquarters at Chicago.

He is a genial gentleman, of fine social qualities, and is counted one of the foremost among Western Underwriters, and is a man of rare and all round ability. His family, father and sons, have represented the Royal for forty-three years.

JOHN HUGH LAW,

Of Law Bros., Managers of the Western Department of the Royal
Insurance Company.

John Hugh Law was born in Savannah, Georgia, August 17th, 1836. His father, Dr. John S. Law, who was one of an old Southern family of English descent, was educated at Yale College, and upon graduating carried off the honors of his class. He removed with his family to Cincinnati about 1848, and here John Hugh commenced his business life, after a liberal education in Herron's College, one of the leading Colleges of its day; also taking a course in a Commercial College. He entered the Insurance office of his father, who in 1852, had been appointed the General Agent of the Royal Insurance Company. Upon the death of Dr. Law, in 1877, the management of the Central Department of the Royal was continued by John H. until 1881, when his two brothers, Charles H. and George W. joined him in the management, with the subject of our sketch as senior member of John H. Law & Bros., and so continued until July of this year, when the firm was chosen by Sub-Manager Beaven and U. S. Manager Beddall to take charge of the Western Department at Chicago, comprising the old territory of the Western and Central Departments, excepting West Virginia.

Mr. Law was married April 20th, 1858, to Miss Georgia Overaker, of Cincinnati. They have six children. He has long been a prominent figure among leading Underwriters and is universally recognized as a gentleman of great executive ability and withal a liberal-minded citizen and a man of the highest integrity. He was for a number of years Mayor of Lenland, Ohio; elected four terms, and served on the Fish and Game Commission of the State of Ohio, appointed first by Gov. Foraker and then by Gov. McKinley.

Mr. Law was one of the original members of the Queen City Club of Cincinnati, and for over twenty years a member of the Currier Club of the same place.

GERALD HENRY LERMIT,

Manager of the Western Department of the Northern Assurance Company of London, England.

Gerald Henry Lermit was born at Dedham, Essex, England, in 1855. At the age of seventeen he joined the staff of the Northern, and some years after, being Assistant Secretary at the Company's London office, the duty was delegated to him of visiting various countries of the world to examine into the Company's business or plant new agencies therein. In this capacity he spent some time in Egypt, India, Burmah, Ceylon, Brazil, the Argentine Republic, Chili, Continental Europe and Canada, as well as the United States, which he visited several times. In 1891 he passed some months inspecting the business of the Northern on the Pacific Coast. On the resignation of Mr. Goodwin and death of Mr. Crooke, in 1894, Mr. Lermit was appointed to succeed them as Manager of the Western Department.

(64)

THEODORE W. LETTON,

General Manager, Prussian National Insurance Company of Germany.

Theodore W. Letton was born July 23d, 1840, near Davenport, Iowa, to which place his parents had moved from Covington, Ky., a few months before. About two years after his parents settled in Quincy, Ill., where they are still living.

He received his education in the private schools of Quincy, and when about eighteen years of age was elected Captain of the Quincy Cadets, a military organization of young men, that afterwards gained the reputation of being one of the best drilled companies in the State.

In September, 1861, he was mustered into service as First Lieutenant, Company C, Fiftieth Illinois Infantry. After serving for a short time on the staff of General B. M. Prentiss in North Missouri, he joined his regiment and took part in the battles of Fort Henry, Donelson and Shiloh. Directly after the latter battle he was promoted to Adjutant, and served in that capacity during the siege and capture of Corinth, which took place the following October. Within a few days following this latter battle, he was detailed as Acting Assistant Adjutant General of the Third Brigade, Second Division, Sixteenth Army Corps, and remained on duty in that position for about eighteen months. While on the Atlanta Campaign he was detailed as Acting Assistant Adjutant General on staff of General Wm. Vandever, who was commanding the troops at Rome, Ga., and performed the duties of that position until the end of his term of service.

After the war Captain Letton settled in Kansas City, Mo., where he engaged in mercantile business for a number of years, and afterwards in the local insurance business.

During the nearly twenty-five years in which Captain Letton has been engaged in fire insurance he has been connected with a number of companies in different capacities. He was for some years Manager of the Western Department of the Fire Association of England, and as a result of his successful handling of the business, was made Manager of the United States Branch of that company, with headquarters in New York City.

He was afterwards Manager of the Western Department of the Union of California, and in 1891, when the Prussian National Insurance Company decided to establish a United States Branch, Captain Letton was appointed General Manager, with headquarters in Chicago.

In February, 1863, Captain Letton was married to Mary C. Field, of Quincy, Ill., and they have three children.

He is a Vestryman of St. Paul's Episcopal Church, Hyde Park; a member of the Loyal Legion, Society of the Army of Tennessee, Grand Army of the Republic, Union League Club, Kenwood Club, and a number of Masonic bodies.

W. J. LITTLEJOHN,

Manager of the Western Department of the North British and Mercantile Insurance Company.

W. J. Littlejohn was born at Memphis, Tenn. He was educated at the University of St. Louis and studied law in that city. He entered the Insurance business in March, '67, in the local agency of the late H. A. Littleton (publishers of Littleton's Digest), at Memphis, Tenn., and afterwards succeeded to the agency business. He continued as a Local Agent at Memphis until 1876, when he was appointed General Agent and Manager at the home office of the Merchants' Insurance Company, of St. Joseph, Mo. This company he conducted with success, largely increasing its surplus and paying handsome dividends, until the change in the home office management of the Connecticut Fire in 1880. Its new president sought out the general agent at St. Joseph, and Mr. Littlejohn became the Connecticut's first supervisor and adjuster in the Western field. In this position he traveled over the entire West, making the acquaintance of the best agents and deriving an experience of great value. As an active member of the Missouri, Kansas & Nebraska State Board, of which he is an ex-president, he took part in the rating of a very wide field and assisted in the establishment of the first Western compact at Kansas City. Soon after the establishment of the Western Department of the Connecticut under Abram Williams in November, '84, Mr. Littlejohn re-insured the Merchants' of St. Joseph in the Connecticut, and it was not long after this that he was called in from the field and made assistant manager of the Connecticut's Western Department, contributing materially to the company's signal success.

ADOLPH LOEB,

United States Manager, North German Fire Insurance of Germany and Trans Atlantic Insurance Company of Germany.

Adolph Loeb was born at Bingen, Germany, on the 9th of March, 1839, receiving his education in the public schools in that country, emigrating to the United States when fifteen years of age. He first engaged in business as a bookkeeper, and later followed mercantile pursuits. In 1870 he started a Fire Insurance Agency, at Memphis, Tenn., with the American Central of St. Louis, Mo., resigning in 1873 to come to Chicago with M. S. Judah, as General Agent of the Manhattan Life Insurance Company, and shortly afterward became General Agent for the Western Department of the Mississippi Valley Fire Insurance Company of Memphis, Tenn. After Mr. Judah's death, he quit the Life Insurance business and continued Fire Insurance alone. He became Manager of the Western Department of the North German Fire Insurance Company, and remained so until it withdrew from this country. He still continued the Local Agency business with his son, Leo A. Loeb, and in 1892 admitted Mr. Louis Becker, his son-in-law. The North German Fire Insurance Company, re-entering the United States in 1892, Mr. Loeb became U. S. Manager of same, deposit made in Illinois.

Mr. Loeb is Secretary of the Commercial Loan and Building Association, which association he started himself in 1883, it now being one of the largest in the State. He is a deacon in Dr. Hirsch's church, a member of the Standard and Lakeside Clubs, a Director of the Bank of Commerce, and of the Michael Reese Hospital and United Hebrew Charities, and also a Director of the Jewish Orphan Asylum at Cleveland, Ohio, and of the Sheltering Home. He was married to Miss Lucille Hart, at Cincinnati, Ohio, in 1864.

J. J. MAYBERRY,

Resident Secretary, Rhode Island Underwriters' Association.

J. J. Mayberry was born at Providence, Rhode Island, in 1868, and was educated in the Public Schools of that city. He entered the Insurance business at Providence, as clerk in the office of the Equitable Fire and Marine Insurance Company, and was appointed to his present position, Resident Secretary of the Rhode Island Underwriters' Association, at Chicago, in 1891. He is a member of the Union League and Ashland Clubs of Chicago.

JOHN J. McDONALD,

General Manager, Western Department, Continental Fire Insurance Company of New York.

John J. McDonald was born in Scotland in 1843 and received his education principally by private tutors. His first business engagement was in the construction of railroads in Europe, afterwards coming to this country and locating in the West. Mr. McDonald entered the insurance business November 12th, 1870, as Local Agent for the Continental Insurance Company in Holt County, Mo. In 1873 he entered the field as Special Agent, covering different states in the West. In 1890 he was transferred to the Pacific Coast and organized that department and took charge as General Agent, continuing until February, 1891, when he was placed in charge of the Western Department as General Manager.

Mr. McDonald was married December 10th, 1872, to Miss M. B. Brown, at Fayette, Mo. They have six children—two boys and four girls.

He is a member of the Masonic fraternity and Union League Club.

CHARLES WRIGHT MEEKER,

Of the Firm of Cox & Meeker.

Charles Wright Meeker was born at Menasha, Wisconsin, January 27th, 1861, and was educated in the public schools of Monroe, Wis. He has had eight years' experience in office and field work and for five years has been Assistant Manager of the Western Department of Underwriters at American Lloyds, New York, and now holds the same position for this and eleven other fire insurance institutions that confine underwriting to selected risks.

Mr. Meeker was married in November, 1888, and has one daughter. He is a 32d degree Mason, a Knight Templar and a member of the Chicago Athletic Club.

GEORGE H. MOORE,

Assistant Secretary, Liverpool & London & Globe Insurance Company.

George H. Moore is a native of New England, and was born in North Hartland, Vermont, January 20th, 1848, being a direct descendant of the Hunt family, who landed in this country in 1835. His early years were spent in Champlain, New York, where he received his education in the academy of that city. At the age of sixteen he commenced earning his own living, clerking in the dry goods store of S. P. Bailey at Plattsburg, New York. In 1866 he moved to Detroit and engaged in the shipping and commission business, forming a copartnership in 1869 with William Livingston, Jr., in a wholesale wood and timber business, in connection with shipping and commission, the company owning four large lake tugs. In 1878 he commenced his career in the Insurance business as Special Agent of the Manhattan Insurance Company, of New York, for Michigan, Ohio, and West Virginia. In 1882 he became connected with the Liverpool and London and Globe as State Agent for Michigan, and January 1st, 1893, was promoted to assistant Resident Secretary of the Chicago branch, covering fifteen States and Territories.

Mr. Moore is a member of the Union League Club, Chicago Whist Club, and Sons of the Revolution. He was married at Detroit, Michigan, December 14th, 1870, to Miss Emma E. Smith, and has six children.

JACOB M. NEUBURGER,

Manager of the Atlas Assurance Company of London.

Jacob M. Neuberger was born at St. Louis, Missouri, on the 4th of July, 1840. He was educated in the common schools of Cincinnati, and commenced business clerking in a dry goods store. He entered the insurance business in 1870, in a local insurance office at Laporte, Indiana, and during 1871 and 1872 was District Agent for the Imperial Insurance Company and Special Agent for the same company until October, 1873, when he was appointed special agent for the German-American Insurance Company, which position he held until August, 1891, when he was appointed Manager of the Atlas Assurance Company, which position he holds at the present time.

Mr. Neuberger was married at Laporte, Indiana, on the 2nd day of January, 1867, and has three children.

He is a member of the Iroquois Club of Chicago, and a Royal Arch Mason.

(72)

DANIEL CONDIT OSMUN,

Resident Manager, Imperial Insurance Company, Limited of London, England.

Daniel Condit Osmun was born at Orange, Essex County, New Jersey, on the 13th of February, 1834. He received his education in the public and private schools of New York City.

He entered the Insurance business in 1849, when he was employed in an office in New York City. He has been connected with various companies since that time, and now holds the position of Resident Manager of the Imperial Insurance Company of London.

Mr. Osmun is a prominent member of the Union League and Washington Park Clubs of Chicago.

ROGERS PORTER,

Assistant Manager, German-American Insurance Company of New York.

Rogers Porter was born at Frome, England, in November, 1843. He entered the Insurance business in 1872, at Cincinnati, with the Phoenix, of Hartford, and in 1873 moved to Chicago, finding employment in the Local Agency office of Mr. James Ayers.

Upon the establishment of the German-American Western Department, he was given a position in the office, and from 1874 to 1888 did special work and adjusting in various portions of the field, receiving the appointment of Assistant Manager in the latter year.

Mr. Porter was married in 1880, at Lewistown, Penn., to Miss Millie C. Long, and has one son. He is a member of the Union League Club and Chicago Athletic Association.

CLARENCE S. PELLET,

Of the Firm of Pellet & Hunter, General Agents.

Clarence S. Pellet was born at Newton, Sussex County, New Jersey, February 26th, 1865, coming to Chicago when quite young. He received his primary education in the common schools and high school of Chicago, and later attended Beloit College, from which he was graduated in the class of 1886.

After leaving college he studied law for a short time at Chicago, and at the death of his father, Oakley B. Pellet, which occurred in January, 1887, he entered the firm of Pellet & Hunter, Local Agents, and has remained connected with the same firm up to the present time.

Mr. Pellet is a member of the Chicago Athletic Association, the Oak Park Club, and the Sigma Chi College Fraternity.

JOHN FOSTER RICE

Assistant Manager, Prussian National Insurance Company of Germany.

John Foster Rice was born February 9th, 1864, in Milwaukee, Wis. He received his early training in that city and after graduating from the academy engaged in the grain commission business on the Milwaukee Board of Trade; a few years later he came to Chicago and entered the employ of S. P. Farrington & Co., wholesale grocers, remaining with them until they retired from business in 1884.

Mr. Rice then entered the Insurance business in the office of E. M. Teall & Co., remaining there until 1887, when he resigned to accept the position of Special Agent for the Fire Insurance Association of England. Later he was appointed Examiner of the Western and Pacific Coast business of the company in their New York office, and in 1889 returned to Chicago as Assistant Manager of the Western Department of the Union of California. In 1891 he was appointed to his present position.

Mr. Rice was married in Chicago in 1887 to Miss Lucy Adelaide Letton. They have three children, all living. He is a member of the Highland Park Club, and Royal Arcanum.

CHARLES RICHARDSON,

Second Assistant General Agent, National Fire Insurance Company of Hartford.

Charles Richardson was born in Indiana on the 19th of July, 1853. He was educated in the public schools and was graduated from Indiana University in 1877. In the latter part of 1877 he entered the law office of Judge Capron to read law and attend to the insurance business of the office. In 1883 he was appointed Special Agent for Indiana of the Franklin Insurance Company, of Indianapolis. In 1884 he went with the Firemens Insurance Company, of Dayton, Ohio, in the capacity of Special Agent and Adjuster, and in 1888 was appointed Secretary and held this position until the Company reinsured in the National of Hartford, Conn., in January, 1892.

In January, 1888, he was married at Greenville, Ohio, to Miss Maude Lecklider. They have two children, a girl and a boy. He is connected with the Sigma Chi College Fraternity, Masonic bodies, Knights Templar, Scottish Rite, 32d degree Mason, and a member of the Medina Temple, Mystic Shrine.

FRANK RITCHIE,

Assistant General Agent, Hanover Fire Insurance Company of New York.

Frank Ritchie was born at Boston, Mass., on the 11th of October, 1852, and received his education in the common schools of Oxford, Ohio. In March, 1872, he entered the Insurance business at Cincinnati, Ohio, in the office of John S. Law & Son, Managers of the Royal Insurance Company, remaining there for twelve years. He was State Agent and Adjuster for the New York Underwriters' Agency for Indiana, with headquarters at Indianapolis, for ten years, from 1884 to 1894; being appointed to his present position, Assistant General Agent of the Hanover Insurance Company, August, 1894, he then removed to Chicago.

JOSEPH MARTIN ROGERS,

Manager of the Western Department of the Queen Insurance Company.

Joseph Martin Rogers was born at Lexington, Kentucky, on the 11th of July, 1839. He attended the Union College at Schenectady, New York, and graduated from the Louisville University Law Department, and later from the Albany, N. Y., Law School. He practiced law at Columbus, Ind., from 1863 to 1866, being Local Agent of the Hartford and Aetna Insurance Companies at the same time. From 1867 to 1868 he was Special Agent of the Hartford; from 1868 to 1871, Local Agent at Louisville; from 1870 to 1875, General Agent for the Central Department of the Imperial; from 1875 to 1876, General Adjuster for the Franklin, of Philadelphia; and from 1876 to 1881, Assistant General Agent for the Phoenix, of New York; he was then appointed to his present position, Manager of the Western Department of the Queen Insurance Company, of Liverpool.

Mr. Rogers was married at Louisville, Ky., to Miss Kate Gamble, December 17th, 1863, and November 21st, 1892, to Miss Julia Rogers, of Chicago, and has five children. He is a member of the University Club, Chicago Literary Club, and an Honorary Member of the Illinois Club.

WILLIAM E. ROLLO,

Of the Firm of W. E. Rollo & Son, General and Local Agents.

William E. Rollo was born in the parish of Gilead, Hebron Township, Tollard County, Connecticut, January 3rd, 1821. After a common school education he became a student at East Windsor Academy, and completed his education at a similar institution at East Hartford, graduating therefrom at the age of eighteen. In 1850 he went to Columbus, Ohio, as a representative of the Hartford Fire Insurance Company, and was also Agent for the Springfield Fire and Marine Insurance Company of Springfield, Mass., the State Mutual of Pennsylvania, and the Connecticut Mutual Life Insurance Company. In 1858 he became General Agent of the Girard Fire and Marine Insurance Company, and during the next two years established agencies in Chicago and all the principal cities of the West. Since 1860 he has been permanently located in Chicago. In 1863 he organized the Merchants' Insurance Company of Chicago. This corporation had become well established and was progressing rapidly, but went down with the great fire of 1871, before the undreamed-of assault upon its assets. The year following that disaster, through Mr. Rollo's efforts, the Traders' Insurance Company was established and made a successful and solid institution. After two years he turned over the enterprise to other parties, and since that time has been engaged in the General and Local Agency business.

Mr. Rollo was married, in October, 1845, to Miss Jane T. Fuller, daughter of General Asa Fuller of Ellington, Connecticut, and has two daughters and a son.

WILLIAM FULLER ROLLO,

Of the Firm of W. C. Rollo & Son, General and Local Agents.

William Fuller Rollo was born at Philadelphia, Pa., February 15th, 1860, removing to Chicago and receiving his education in that city. May 1st, 1877, he became identified with the Insurance business, and has remained in this connection up to the present time. January 31st, 1882, he was married to Miss Mary Rice Smith of Conneaut, Ohio.

SAMUEL A. ROTHERMEL

Assistant Secretary, Traders' Insurance Company.

Samuel A. Rothermel was born January 1st, 1849, at New Berlin, Pa., and comes of good old Holland stock. His education was received in the common schools at Jersey Shore, Pa., and at West Branch Academy of the same place. Making his way westward, he entered the service of the Adams Insurance Company of Freeport, Illinois, in 1866, as an office boy, and in 1867 was employed in the local agency of the Aetna at that place. During 1868 he was in the dry goods and grocery business at Morris, Illinois, but in 1869 he went with H. S. Tiffany & Co.'s Insurance Agency as Office and Special Agent, remaining until 1871.

He then engaged in merchant tailoring at Elgin, Illinois, but returned to Insurance in 1873 as Local Agent at Kansas City. In the following year he became connected with the Traders of this city and has remained with it continuously in various capacities ever since. Thus, since 1866, with the exception of two years, he has been in the Insurance ranks, always doing good work. Mr. Rothermel was also President of the Chicago Underwriters' Association for two years, and is prominent in civic affairs, having served one term as President of the town of Cicero, and for ten years Treasurer of the Oak Park Building Association. He has also been Secretary and Treasurer of the Oak Park Land Association and President of the River Forest Land Company. He has taken an interest in military affairs, for five years was an officer of the First Regiment, Illinois National Guard. He is a man widely known, and as widely respected for his sterling qualities.

A. F. SHAW,

Chief Clerk of Goodwin, Hall & Henshaw.

A. F. Shaw, Chief Clerk of Goodwin, Hall & Henshaw, was born at Manchester, England, January 29th, 1866.

Mr. Shaw was educated privately and commenced his business career by entering the office of his father, a leading coal merchant and insurance agent of his native city. At the age of 17 he joined his elder brother in Chicago, and secured a junior position with the Springfield Fire and Marine in its office in Chicago. Mr. Shaw made some changes, all in the way of promotions, serving a short time in the Lancashire and four years in the Connecticut offices. Upon the establishment of the Western Department of the Anglo-Nevada, Mr. Shaw was selected as Cashier by Manager S. T. Collins, who was not slow to recognize the gentleman's ability and advanced him very shortly to the position of Chief Clerk, which position he continued to fill with the Caledonian after the reinsurance of the Anglo-Nevada by that company. Declining to go to Philadelphia on the discontinuance of the Western Department at Chicago, Mr. Shaw entered the local business with first agencies of the Grand Rapids of Michigan and Alamo of Texas on November 1st, 1891. Mr. Shaw continued to represent the companies named as First Agent, and the Traders of Chicago, Union of London, and Sun of England as Second Agent until in May, 1894, he was induced by Messrs. Goodwin, Hall & Henshaw to accept a flattering proposal to enter their office as Chief Clerk. Mr. Shaw has especial charge of the Local Agency of the firm, the principal's time being devoted more particularly to the extensive General Agency of the Union and other companies represented.

Mr. Shaw married, January 29th, 1891, Mary Emma Moore, a Chicago lady, and is the father of two children, a boy and a girl.

(83)

CHARLES G. SHEPARD,

Assistant Manager of the Queen Insurance Company of America.

Charles G. Shepard was born at Columbus, Ohio, on the 15th of November, 1852, and was educated in the public schools of that place. After finishing his education he entered the County Auditor's office, and in January, 1871, began his Insurance career with the Home Insurance Company of Columbus, Ohio.

In January, 1882, he came to Chicago to accept a position with the Western Department of the Queen Insurance Company, with which company he is still connected.

Mr. Shepard, in 1887, married a Miss Blend of Oneonta, New York. They have one child, a son.

JOHN SHEPHERD,

General Agent, Manchester Fire Assurance Company of Manchester, England.

John Shepherd was born in Carroll County, Tennessee, July 29th, 1849, of English and Scotch descent. He was educated in a private school and at Cumberland University, Lebanon, Tennessee, being a graduate of the class of 1870. He entered life as a lawyer, practiced eight years, then did general business until entering the General Agency business at Chicago, Illinois, in March, 1883, in the Loss Department of the North British and Mercantile Insurance Company. He was married, August 16th, 1870, to Miss Mary E. Sharp of Macon, Mo., and has one son, J. E. Shepherd. His family is one of the oldest of English and Scotch extraction in America, his parental ancestors coming with the first permanent colony to Virginia in 1607. All of his great-grandparents were patriots in the Revolution, two of them being distinguished officers in the army. Though Southern by birth, his father and mother were staunch Union people in the Rebellion, when it counted much for one to love country above property and faction. Few families suffered or endured more for real Union than his, to whom the American flag was an emblem of the glory of an indivisible Union of independent States. The Union, the Constitution, the enforcement of the law, was the platform upon which they stood in that severest test of real patriotism in America.

Mr. Shepherd is a Free Mason, being a member of the Garfield Lodge, No. 643, York Chapter, No. 148, Columbia Commandery, No. 63, Oriental Consistory, Scottish Rite, thirty-second degree.

ROBERT J. SMITH,

Secretary, Traders' Insurance Company, of Chicago, Illinois.

Robert Jordan Smith was born near Belleville, Illinois, June 12th, 1837. Mr. Smith prides himself in being a descendant of one of St. Clair County's earliest settlers. He attended the public schools in his neighborhood until about fifteen years old, when he entered Shurtleff College. He remained there a few months, when he left to engage in teaching. In 1860 Mr. Smith began his Insurance career as a Local Agent for the Aetna at Red Bud, Illinois. While there he was occasionally called upon to do some special work for the company. A State Agency for the Aetna was given him in 1865, which soon occasioned his removing to Springfield. This continued for two years, when he was appointed General Agent for the Western Department of the Putnam Insurance Company of Hartford, with headquarters at Chicago. The great Chicago fire of 1871 bankrupted the Putnam, and so left him to engage elsewhere. The North British and Mercantile soon after appointed him Superintendent of Agencies, covering Illinois, Iowa, Missouri and Minnesota. A little later the New Orleans Insurance Association appointed him its Northwestern General Agent, for which and all companies he, ever represented he rendered efficient service, and was most successful in the field. In 1874 the Traders Insurance Company of Chicago was in need of a competent man for Secretary. Mr. Smith was chosen for that position, and has remained with the company ever since, and has brought to the Traders distinct success. Mr. Smith has always taken the most active and faithful interest in different underwriting organizations. He has been Supervising Agent of the National Board; always a leader in the affairs of the Fire Underwriters' Association of the Northwest, and was its honored President in 1873; was President of the International Board of Inland Marine Underwriters in 1876. He took an active and prominent part in the formation of the Union, and has always been one of its most loyal supporters and counselors. Mr. Smith has filled every position of trust and honor in the different Fire Insurance organizations, as well as served upon their Boards of Directors and Executive high position of honor and trust at the last meeting, held at Niagara.
Committees, and he is at present the President of the Western Union, being called to that

JOHN V. THOMAS,

Assistant Resident Secretary, Liverpool & London & Globe Insurance
Company.

John V. Thomas was born and educated in Princeton, N. J. Came West in 1857, and settled during the summer of that year in Dixon, Ill. His first commission as an Insurance Agent was received in 1865, though real estate required the greater part of his attention until 1874, when he engaged regularly in the insurance business, and the leading Agency in his adopted city was the result. In the fall of 1881 he received the appointment of State Agent for Illinois for the Liverpool and London and Globe Insurance Company, which position he successfully filled until called to his present position, January 1st, 1893. His twelve years of field work show him to be closely identified, and always in harmony, with the Illinois State Board of Fire Underwriters, which he served as its President, as a member of its Executive Committee and one of its District Chairmen. He is at present a member of this organization and is also a member of the Fire Association of the Northwest. His adopted city bears many evidences of his interest in its welfare; his activity in securing many public improvements being aided by his prominence in city affairs during two years as Alderman and five consecutive terms as Mayor.

He is a Knight Templar and a 32d degree Mason.

HENRY H. WALKER,

Secretary, Western Farm Department and Illinois State Agent of the
Home of New York.

Henry H. Walker was born in Rush County, Indiana, in 1839. While engaged in merchandising, at the age of twenty, he wrote his first insurance policy, which was for the Aetna, under the late J. B. Bennett. From the age of twenty to twenty-five he represented as Local Agent, in addition to the Aetna, the Phoenix of Hartford, the Hartford, the Old Manhattan, and the Security of New York. At the age of twenty-five he entered the employ of the Security as a Special Agent, in Illinois, and continued for one year, when he engaged with the Home of New York as an Adjuster, traveling out from New York city. On January 1st, 1867, he took charge of the Home's State Agency in Indiana, and continued until July, 1887. He removed permanently from Indiana on July 1st, 1887, to assume the management of the Home's Western Farm Department at Chicago, to which, in October, 1893, the Sub-Agency Mercantile business of the Western States was added; and November 1st, 1894, the general supervision of the company's entire business in the State of Illinois was also placed in his hands.

WILLIAM SEYMOUR WARREN,

Resident Secretary, Chicago Branch of the Liverpool & London & Globe Insurance Company.

William Seymour Warren was born at Cleveland, Ohio, May 10th, 1848, and is a son of the late William Warren, who was Resident Secretary from 1875 to the time of his death in November, 1889. Mr. Warren was educated in the high schools of Cincinnati, and entered the Insurance business as an office boy at Chicago, December 3rd, 1866. He was City Manager of the Liverpool & London & Globe at Chicago when his father died, and was appointed, together with Mr. George Crooke, to succeed him. Mr. Crooke withdrew in December, 1892, leaving Mr. Warren sole Secretary. His entire business life, from his school days to the present time, has been devoted to the service of the Liverpool & London & Globe Insurance Company.

Mr. Warren was married at Chicago, January 4th, 1883, to Miss Fannie R. Parsons, and has two children, a boy and girl. He is a member of the Union League Club of Chicago.

CLINTON WEEKS,

General Agent of the Norwood Insurance Company of New York.

Clinton Weeks was born at New London, Conn., March 10th, 1866. After leaving school he was employed as a clerk in the office of the United States Life Insurance Company at New London, and in 1885, entered the Fire Insurance business at Chicago. He was married at Chicago, to Miss Edith Fairfield, and has three children. Is a member of the Chicago Athletic Club and Harvard Club of Englewood.

JOSEPH L. WHITLOCK,

Western Manager of the Glens Falls Insurance Company.

Joseph L. Whitlock was born at Mendham, New Jersey, June 10th, 1849. He was educated at Chester Institute, Morris County, New Jersey. At the age of eighteen years he came to Chicago and found employment in the office of Moore & Steans, 49 LaSalle Street, the largest fire insurance agency in Chicago. Afterwards he became connected with the Commercial Fire of this city, as Inspector. In 1869 he was elected Secretary of the National Fire of Chicago. In 1872 he joined the staff of the local agency of Mr. C. H. Case, and subsequently was appointed Special Agent and Adjuster of the Royal, under the management of Mr. Case. Here he remained until 1882, when he assumed his present position.

Mr. Whitlock has taken a prominent part in Western Fire Underwriters' organizations. He has served as President of the Illinois State Board, and in 1885 was President of the Fire Underwriters' Association of the Northwest. He is a believer in and advocate of sound practices in fire underwriting, which he enforces in the conduct of his own business.

He is quite active outside of insurance, in business, political and social life. He is a stanch Prohibitionist and the party has honored him on several occasions with nominations for public office. He has been their candidate for alderman, mayor and member of Congress. He is a member of the Young Men's Christian Association and was its treasurer in 1883-5. He is also active in church and Sunday School, being an officer of the Emmanuel M. E. church, Evanston, Ill., and Superintendent of its Sunday School. He is a fluent speaker and his voice is always heard on the side of morality and right.

CHARLES LEWIS WHITTEMORE.

With the Western Department, North British and Mercantile Insurance
Company.

Charles Lewis Whittemore was born at Belchertown, Mass., May 15th, 1859. He was educated in the public schools of Springfield, Mass., and at Amherst College, Amherst, Mass. He entered the office of the Connecticut Fire Insurance Company in 1880, was connected with the Providence-Washington in 1892. and with the North British & Mercantile Insurance Company in 1895.

He was married Jan. 1st, 1884, at Springfield, Mass., to Miss Lillia E. Wilson, and has one child. He is a member of the Union League Club and the Chicago Athletic Association.

ABRAM WILLIAMS,

Manager, Western Department of the Connecticut Fire Insurance Company.

Abram Williams was born at Utica, New York. March 31st, 1830. At the age of fourteen his father died, and he was obliged to leave school and make his own way in the world. His career commenced as clerk in a store, later engaging in business on his own account, and in 1855 he established a mercantile house in New York with connections at Paris, France. He enlisted in the Union Army in 1862, and served successively as Lieutenant in the Sixth Iowa Cavalry, as chief of Cavalry on General Sully's staff, and as Assistant Quartermaster, with the rank of Major. Returning from the war, Major Williams established a Local Insurance Agency at Dubuque, Iowa, afterwards becoming Special State and General Agent of the Yonkers Fire of New York. In 1869 he was appointed Western Manager of the Company, and came to Chicago. The Company suffered by the Chicago fire of 1871, and in a courageous attempt to save the books of his office he was seriously injured and crippled for two years. In 1874 he was able to resume active work, and was appointed Superintendent of the Farm Department of the west for the Continental, of New York. Mr. Williams remained with this Company until October, 1884, when he became Manager of the Western Department of the Connecticut Fire, which position he still occupies. He has served one term as President of the Fire Underwriters' Association of the Northwest, and is well and favorably known in social circles; is a member of the Union League Club and a Knight Templar.

(93)

CONRAD WITKOWSKY,

Of the Firm of Witkowsky & Affold. General Agents.

Conrad Witkowsky was born at Posen, Prussia, on the 2d of December, 1839. His parents came to America when he was very young and he received his education in the public schools of New York and Chicago. After leaving High School he engaged in mercantile business with his father at Chicago, resigning in 1866 to enter the office of S. M. Moore & Co., Insurance Agents of Chicago, which firm was dissolved some years later.

Mr. Witkowsky was married at Chicago in 1864, to a lady who bore the same name as himself; they have three children.

He is a member of the Standard and Lakeside Clubs, Masonic and other fraternities.

MORITZ WOLF,

General Agent, German Fire Insurance Company of Peoria, Illinois.

Moritz Wolf was born in Austria on the 24th of August, 1864. He received his education in the public schools of his native country, and studied Law for about two years. He came to this country when quite a young man and in 1884 entered the Insurance business at Chicago, Ill., in a Local Agency office.

Mr. Wolf was married May 26th, 1891, to Miss Minnie Hartwig, of Watertown, Wis. They have two children.

JOHN O. WRIGHT,

Superintendent of Agencies, Hanover Fire Insurance Company of New York.

John O. Wright was born at Covington, Kentucky, in the year 1856, and was educated in the public schools of Cincinnati. He commenced business as cashier and bookkeeper in a hat and fur store in Cincinnati, and entered the Insurance business in the summer of 1875 as a clerk in the office of John S. Law & Son, Cincinnati, coming to Chicago in 1882 as Daily Report Examiner for the Western Department of the Springfield Fire and Marine Insurance Company. He was Special Agent for that company for Ohio in 1883 and 1884, and was in a similar capacity for the New York Underwriters in 1885 and Cook County Special Agent for the same company from 1886 until the organization of the Western Department of the Hanover Insurance Company.

(96)

Adjusters,
State and Special Agents,
Etc.

GEORGE W. ADAMS,

General Adjuster.

Geo. W. Adams was born at Tiffin, Ohio, on the 31st of May, 1843, and received his education in a country log school house. He worked on a farm until fifteen years of age, when he obtained a position in a bank. May 1st, 1867, he engaged in Fire Insurance business at Tiffin, Ohio.

Mr. Adams was married in 1863 to Miss Rogers and has one child living. He is a member of the Union League Club of Chicago.

SHERWOOD DICKERSON ANDRUS,

Special Agent, Providence Washington Insurance Company of Providence, R. I.

Sherwood Dickerson Andrus was born in Watertown, Jefferson County, New York, April 5th, 1855; was educated in the public schools of his native city, with the exception of when he attended Hope College, of Holland, Michigan. Engaged in business for the first time in 1871, in the book and stationery store of Messrs. Hanford & Wood, in Watertown, and in the following spring, with his father, Mr. Merritt M. Andrus, in the grocery and produce business, which occupation he followed until October, 1872, when he entered the insurance business with the "Black River," afterwards known as the Northern Insurance Company of New York, with headquarters in Watertown. He remained with that company until June, 1878, when he resigned to accept a situation as Assistant Cashier in the wholesale grocery house of Messrs. Sprague, Warner & Co., of Chicago. In February, 1879, he went to Leadville, Colo., and engaged in the fancy grocery business, which occupation he followed until the next November, when he became actively engaged in silver mining, and continued in that until May, 1883, when he returned to Chicago and entered the wholesale dry goods house of Messrs. Cleveland, Cummings & Woodruff, as Assistant Credit man. Upon the collapse of that house, the following November, he concluded to return permanently to the Insurance business and in April, 1884, he connected himself with the Sun Fire Office of England, as Special Agent for Illinois, under Col. Thomas Johnston, who was then its State Agent; he continued with that company until the spring of 1886, when he resigned to accept a position with the Mississippi Valley and Northwestern Mutual Fire Insurance Companies of Rock Island, Ill., under Mr. David S. Wagner. In the following August he resigned to accept a position as Special Agent for the Norwich Union Fire Insurance Society of England, for the States of Illinois and Indiana. While engaged with this Society he was three times elected to fill the position of Secretary of the Illinois State Board of Fire Underwriters, with which organization he has been identified ever since. In May, 1890, he resigned from the Norwich Union to accept a position of Daily Report Examiner in the General Western Insurance office in Chicago of the National Fire Insurance Company of Hartford, Conn., which position he filled until May, 1893, when he again resigned to accept the position of Chief Clerk in the General Western office of the company he is now associated with. He is a member of the Auburn Park, Ill., Blue Lodge and Chapter, A. F. and A. M., and Fidelity Council of the Royal League of Normal Park, Ill.

CHARLES GERRY AYARS,

Illinois State Agent, Phoenix Insurance Company of Hartford, Conn.

Charles Gerry Ayars was born at Newton, New Jersey, on the 28th of December, 1831. He received his education in private schools and the grammar school of Rutgers College, New Jersey. His father, the Rev. James Ayars, was a Methodist minister, in active service for fifty years. Two of his brothers were officers in the Union army, the youngest being killed at the battle of Petersburg. After leaving school Mr. Ayars engaged in the produce business at Jersey City, N. J. In the spring of 1857 he came West and went to Covington, Ky. In 1858-59 was in the office of the Western Department of the Phoenix Insurance Company of Hartford, at Cincinnati, Ohio. Came to Evanston, Ills., in 1859, and engaged in farming until 1874. He was County Commissioner of Cook County from 1875 to 1881, and in 1882 went with the Phoenix as Special Agent.

Mr. Ayars was married, in 1859, to Margaret H. Fredinburg of New York city. He is a member of the Evanston Masonic Lodge, Evanston Chapter and Evanston Commandery, the Evanston Club and the Evanston Boat Club.

WILLIAM N. BAMENT,

Special Agent and Adjuster, Home Insurance Company of New York.

William N. Bament was born at Cincinnati, Ohio, on October 19th, 1858. He received his education in the Grammar and High Schools of Cincinnati, and entered the Insurance business at Cincinnati, May 2d, 1876, with the Insurance Adjustment Company, remaining with them for seven years. In September, 1883, he entered the service of the California Insurance Company of San Francisco, and served in the capacity of correspondent, head of the Loss Department and Special Agent. In November, 1886, he was appointed General Agent of the Central Department of the California Insurance Company, with headquarters at Cincinnati, holding said position until the retirement of the Company in 1892. Since that time he has been with the Home Insurance Company of New York as Special Agent and Adjuster, with headquarters at Chicago.

Mr. Bament was married at Cincinnati, Ohio, June 30th, 1886, to Miss Ida L. Vaughn and has two children.

JAMES G. S. BEST,

Special Agent, Agricultural Insurance Company of Watertown, N. Y.

James G. S. Best was born at Blairsville, Pennsylvania, on the 25th of January, 1846. In September, 1863, he entered the Insurance field at Freeport, Illinois, and with the exception of two years this has been his only business.

He was with the American, Continental and United States Insurance Companies, all of Freeport, then called the "Hartford of the West." Came to Chicago in 1873, and was with the American of Chicago until it re-insured in 1883. He then became connected with the Agricultural Insurance Company of Watertown, N. Y., as Special Agent for the ten states comprising their Western field, and still fills that position

JOSEPH L. BIERBRAUER,

Special Agent of the Rochester German Insurance Company.

Joseph L. Bierbrauer was born at Rochester, N. Y., in the same house as his father, who was prominent in politics, having served three terms in the Common Council and being a delegate to State and National conventions on several occasions, and died, having still another year to serve as member of the Common Council. Joseph L. was educated in the Rochester Public Schools, the German Parochial School and the Rochester Business College. He entered the Fire Insurance business in Rochester, N. Y., in 1886, and has been employed since 1890 by the Rochester German Insurance Company. He was married at Rochester, in April, 1893, to Miss Rose Knipper, and has one child, a daughter.

Mr. Bierbrauer is an honorary member of the Ancient Order of Foresters of America and the Court Pride of Flower City at Rochester.

J. P. BLACK,

General Adjuster.

Mr. Black is a native of Ohio. He has been a resident of Chicago since the first of January, 1867, and from that date until the time of this sketch has been prominent as an Adjuster of fire losses. He has been concerned mainly in cases where large interests were involved and his treatment of these has been such as to call forth hearty commendation from the Companies interested.

WAITE BLIVEN,

Special Agent of the American Fire Insurance Company of Philadelphia.

Waite Bliven was born at Cincinnati, Ohio, June 29th, 1867. He was educated in the public schools of Toledo, Ohio, and entered the Fire Insurance business at the same place in the Western Department office of the Howard Insurance Company of New York. In 1885 he came to Chicago and was appointed Special Agent of The American Fire Insurance Company, which position he holds at the present time.

October 2d, 1890, Mr. Bliven was married at Chicago, to Miss Gertrude Foster, and has one child—Charles Foster Bliven.

THOMAS ANTHONY BOWDEN,

Superintendent of Ratings, Chicago Underwriters' Association.

Thomas Anthony Bowden was born in Boston, Mass., June 21st, 1845, and received a thorough education in the schools of that city. He commenced business as packer for a manufacturer of millinery goods and in 1872 became connected with the Chicago Board of Underwriters.

Mr. Bowden was married at Portsmouth, New Hampshire, to Miss A. P. Ferguson, and has two children. He is a member of the Masonic Fraternity, Royal Arcanum, Grand Army of the Republic, Royal League and National Union.

WILLIAM DAVID BRADSHAW,

General Agent of the Union Insurance Company of Philadelphia.

William David Bradshaw was born at Bolivar, Ohio, on the 3d of January, 1851. He attended the High School at Lockport, New York, and later the High School at Freeport, Illinois. In 1867 he commenced his business career in the office of the American Insurance Company at Freeport, Illinois. For fifteen years he was with the American Insurance Company, of Chicago; for four years he was Assistant Manager to Mr. C. H. Case, Manager of the Royal and the London and Lancashire Insurance Companies, and in 1886 was appointed General Agent for the Union, of Philadelphia, in the Western field.

In 1878 Mr. Bradshaw was married to Miss Mabel Hickcox, and has one child.

GRANT R. BROWN,

Special Agent, Western Department of the Pennsylvania Fire Insurance Company of Philadelphia.

Mr. Brown was born in Racine, Wis., on the 9th day of February, 1864; was educated in Racine and Chicago Public Schools, and commenced his insurance career in the office of the Hartford Fire Insurance Company under G. F. Bissell, General Agent, in 1884, remaining with them nearly eight years, resigning to accept the position of Daily Report Examiner for Wm. C. Brown, then General Agent Western Department of the German Insurance Company of Quincy, Ill.; afterward becoming Special Agent for the Royal Insurance Company, Case & Co., Managers, and Chief Clerk in office for same Company. Mr. Brown was married in Chicago in July, 1887, to Miss Maude A. Furness, and has two boys. He is a member of the Royal League.

WILLIAM C. BROWN,

Special Agent and Adjuster, Pennsylvania Fire Insurance Company of Philadelphia.

William C. Brown was born at Racine, Wisconsin, August 31st, 1861, being educated in the Public Schools of that place. He started his business career with the Hartford Fire Insurance Company at 49 La Salle Street, Chicago, August 31st, 1875, and was with them until April 1st, 1884; from that time until December, 1889, he was in the Local business in St. Paul, Minn.; then General Agent of the German Insurance Company of Quincy, Illinois, until it re-insured in 1893. He has been with the Pennsylvania Fire Insurance Company since the opening of the Chicago General Office.

Mr. Brown was married in Chicago to Miss Ionia E. Lovett and has two children.

J. MABBETT BROWN,

General Adjuster.

John Mabbett Brown was born in New York City March 30th, 1829. After an academic education he came West in 1845, and in 1846 entered a general merchandise store at Battle Creek, Mich. In 1850 he moved to Michigan City, where he was employed as bookkeeper and cashier in the commission business. From there he returned to New York in 1851 and served a clerkship as General Average Adjuster with the Atlantic Mutual Marine Insurance Company of New York. In 1854 Mr. Brown was injured on the Long Island Railroad, compelling him to retire from business for two years. He then came to Chicago, and for three years was a member of the Chicago Board of Trade. Returning again to New York City in 1857, he traveled from there through the Southern States, selling goods, until the Rebellion broke out, when he joined the army and served until the close of the war in 1865. From that time until 1869 he was engaged in the Local Insurance business at Toledo, Ohio, during which time he traveled through the State of Michigan, doing special work for the Putnam Fire Insurance Company of Hartford, Conn. In October, 1871, he was appointed State Agent for the Continental Insurance Company of New York, for Michigan, remaining with that company until 1875, when he joined the field forces of the North British and Mercantile, under the management of Lewis and Cornell, and later in the same year received an appointment with the Traders Insurance Company as General Adjuster. February 1st, 1877, he was appointed Special Agent for the Northwest of the Imperial and Northern Insurance Company, under the management of R. D. Alliger, Resident Manager, and D. C. Osmun, Superintendent of Agencies, and remained with them until September 1st, 1895.

Mr. Brown was married to Miss Elizabeth Gabriella O'Brien in 1858, in Brooklyn, New York and has one son and one daughter. He is a member of the Chicago Athletic Association and Apollo Commandery.

(112)

ROBERT B. CARSON,

Special Agent, Commercial Union Assurance Company.

Robert B. Carson was born in Holmes County, Ohio, September 25th, 1832, and received his education in the Public Schools of Illinois. He entered the grain and commission business in the fall of 1856, continuing in said business until the fall of 1862. April 12th, 1863, he commenced the Insurance business in Indiana, and after many and various changes in career, we now find him Special Agent for the Commercial Union Assurance Company at Chicago. June 19th, 1859, he was married to Miss Lina A. Pond. They have two children. He is a member of the Masonic order and the Grand Calumet Height Gun Club.

HENRY W. CARLISLE,

Special Agent, Continental Insurance Company of New York.

Henry W. Carlisle was born at Chicago, Illinois, March 28th, 1862, receiving his education in the Public Schools of that place.

In 1875 he entered the Insurance business in Chicago and spent eighteen months as office boy with I. J. Lewis; six months with the Atlas Insurance Company of Hartford; eight years with R. S. Critchell & Co., as boy clerk and bookkeeper; seven years with the Liverpool & London & Globe Insurance Company, as Cashier and City Manager; two years as Special Agent in Illinois for the Providence Washington Insurance Company, of Providence, R. I., and sixteen months as Special Agent for the Continental Insurance Company of New York, for Chicago and Cook County.

E. G. CARLISLE,

Special Agent, Springfield Fire and Marine Insurance Company.

(115)

JAMES H. CASWELL,

General Adjuster, Western Department of the Germania Fire Insurance
Company of New York.

James H. Caswell was born in Columbia County, New York, March 22d, 1853, receiving his education in the public schools and at Wymanock Seminary, New Lebanon, New York.

He commenced his business life in 1870 as clerk in a grocery store at Pittsfield, Mass., shortly after coming west and engaging in the dry goods trade. Later he was employed for three years in the Government Mail service. In 1877 he entered the Local Insurance field. In 1881 he commenced traveling for the Orient Insurance Company, of Hartford, and in 1884 for the Germania. November 29th, 1884, he was married at Minneapolis. Minn., to Lizzie H. Frazier.

(116)

S. E. CATE,

Special Agent and General Adjuster, Delaware and Reliance Insurance
Companies of Philadelphia.

Stephen E. Cate was born in London, England, in 1857, of Scotch and English parents, and came to this country when a mere lad. After graduating at the Des Moines High School in 1876, he entered the employ of the Hawkeye Insurance Company, of Des Moines, Iowa, as office boy, and after a thorough office training was promoted to Special Agent and remained in that capacity until the organization of the Globe Insurance Company, when he accepted the position of State Agent and Adjuster, and remained with them until the company sold its business to another organization.

Mr. Cate then accepted the position of Adjuster in the Western field for the Phenix, of Brooklyn, continuing in their service in that capacity for four years. He was then tendered the position of Special Agent and Adjuster by Henry E. Bowers, Manager of the Guardian, of London, for six Western States, which position he retained until the organization of the Western Department of the Delaware and Reliance. He then accepted the position of Special Agent and General Adjuster for the field controlled by that department, which position he now occupies.

Mr. Cate is an old "National Guardsman" with rank of Colonel, and was on the staff of Governor Sherman for four years. He is a Knight Templar, Shriner and Thirty-second degree Mason, and a member of the Episcopal Church. He is married and has one son, Lester, now attending Military School at Mobile, Alabama.

(117)

CHARLES T. CHANDLER,

Special Agent, National Fire Insurance Company of Hartford, Conn.

Charles T. Chandler was born at Galena, Illinois, and at the age of eight years came with his parents to Chicago, receiving his education in the Public Schools of that city. He entered the Fire Insurance business in 1877, under W. B. Cornell, Superintendent of the North British and Mercantile Insurance Company, remaining with this Company four years; was then two years in the General Agency office of the Phenix of Brooklyn, also with the Niagara General Agency for about a year, leaving to accept a position as Assistant of Inspections and Rating, for the Minneapolis Board of Underwriters, where he remained about a year. Returning to Chicago in 1885, Mr. Chandler engaged as Inspector for the Chicago Fire Underwriters' Association, until appointed Superintendent of the Cook County Compact. He held this position for over four years, until illness compelled his resignation. In September, 1889, he was appointed Special Agent for Cook County, for the National Fire Insurance Company of Hartford, which position he still holds.

Mr. Chandler was married in 1893 at Mineral Point, Wis., and has one child, a daughter. He is Secretary of Cook County Fieldmen's Association, also a Director of the Ashland Club of Chicago.

SAMUEL T. COCKEY,

Special Agent, Allemania Fire Insurance Company of Pittsburg, Pa.

Samuel T. Cockey was born at Norfolk, Litchfield County, Conn., August 16th, 1847. He received his education in the District Schools of Connecticut and finished at Christomatic Institute, Rye, Westchester County, New York.

Mr. Cockey first engaged in business at West Winstead, Conn., in a Country Store. He moved to Chicago in 1872 and entered the Insurance business as State Agent of the Lycoming Insurance Co. of Pennsylvania, and later became a member of the firm of Geo. P. Treadway & Co., General and Local Agents. In 1884 Mr. Cockey retired from the firm and Mr. Treadway continued the business. Mr. Cockey then engaged in the Brokerage business until 1888, when he accepted the position which he now holds with the Allemania.

GEORGE C. COOPER,

State Agent for Michigan and Wisconsin for the Fireman's Fund Insurance Company of California.

Geo. C. Cooper was born at Waterloo, Seneca County, N. Y., January 29th, 1841. His education was obtained in the common schools and at Falley Seminary, Fulton, Oswego County, N. Y., where he was thoroughly prepared for business, which he entered as clerk in a grocery store; afterward he was employed in a general store, and for twelve years was in business for himself. In 1876 he entered the Insurance business at Sturgis, Mich., and in 1877 commenced to travel for the Firem n's Fund Insurance Company as State Agent for Michigan, and in 1890 added Wisconsin to his field, with headquarters at the Company's General Agency, 153 La Salle street, Chicago.

Mr. Cooper was married at Fulton, N. Y., May 13th, 1869, to Miss Louise A. Warner; has two daughters living, Mrs. Jay A. Pearsall and Mrs. Sam B. Taylor, of Lansing, Mich.

GEORGE CROOKE,

Manager, Western Adjustment and Inspection Company of Chicago

George Crooke was born at Hebden Bridge, Yorkshire, England, November 27th, 1828, and was educated in private schools. He was first engaged in the mercantile business, came to the United States in 1850, served as a private soldier, and later as First Lieutenant and Adjutant of the Twenty-first Regiment, Iowa Volunteer Infantry, from 1862 to 1865. He entered the Insurance business in 1866 at McGregor, Iowa, served as Local Agent and as Special Agent of the Hartford Fire Insurance Company, and as Special Agent and Associate Manager of the Chicago Branch of the Liverpool & London & Globe Insurance Company.

In 1856, at Pecatonica, Mo., he was married to Mrs. Jane Lloyd, and has three children. He is a Mason, a member of the I. O. O. F., and the Military Order of the Loyal Legion.

JACOB C. DIETZ

Special Agent and Adjuster of the Traders' Insurance Company.

Jacob C. Dietz is a native of New York, and was born at Oneonta, Otsego County. He was educated in the Common and Select Schools of his native County, and when in his teens became a clerk in a country store for C. P. Huntington, now so famous in connection with the Southern Pacific and other railroads. Later on, he studied law, and in 1862 emigrated to Iowa and soon after became deputy in the office of the Clerk of the District Court of Jones County. He was afterward elected Clerk, serving four terms. In 1868 he was admitted to the bar and from 1874 to 1893 was to some extent engaged in the practice of law, making Insurance cases a specialty. In 1867 he engaged in the Insurance business at Anamosa and for some thirteen years has been Special Agent and Adjuster for the Traders, coming to Chicago to work from the head office in 1884, where he has proved a valuable acquisition to the Company. He has been prominent in church and social circles and an influential factor in Iowa politics in his county. He was Mayor of Anamosa two terms and for eight years was Chairman of the Republican Committee of his County. He is a member of the Masonic Fraternity and of the Odd Fellows and a genial companion in private life.

HENRY A DIKE,

Special Agent of the Fire Association of Philadelphia.

Henry A. Dike was born in New York City, N. Y., on the 20th of April, 1855; was educated at Barre Academy, Barre, Vermont. From 1875 to 1876, he engaged in mercantile pursuits in New York; from 1877 to 1878 was in the lumber trade; from 1878 to 1879 was in the railroad business in Colorado, and in 1880 entered the Fire Insurance business in the office of W. H. Cunningham, Manager of the Fire Association of Philadelphia, of which Company he is now Special Agent.

Mr. Dike was married at Barre, Vermont, August 23d, 1882, to Miss Fanny D. Carleton, and has two daughters.

BENJAMIN B. DOW,

Special Agent. Queen Insurance Company of America.

Benjamin B. Dow was born in Orange County, New York, Sept. 23d, 1849, receiving his education in the Northwestern College, at Plainsfield, Ill. Raised on a farm, his early days were spent in agricultural pursuits; later he was engaged in telegraphing, railroading, general merchandising, banking, grain and commissions, and in 1874 entered the Insurance field at Dwight, Ill.

October 3d, 1872, he was married at Dwight, Ill., to Miss Mary J. Devoe, and has two daughters. He is a member of the I. O. O. F. Lodge, Dwight, Ill.

ELMER W. DREHER,

Special Agent. Spring Garden Insurance Company of Philadelphia.

Elmer W. Dreher was born at Tamaqua, Pennsylvania, October 2d, 1862, and was educated in the Public Schools of Freeport, Illinois. He commenced in the Insurance business in January, 1883, entering the General Agency Office of the Rhode Island Underwriters' Association at Chicago. January, 1885, he went to Bloomington, Illinois, as Assistant to the Manager of the Central Illinois Compact. October, 1885, he returned to Chicago and entered the General Agency office of the Providence Washington Insurance Company, and October, 1886, became Special Agent for the same Company. In May, 1893, he was appointed Special Agent of the Spring Garden Insurance Company for the Northwestern States, which position he held until his appointment to a position in the Home office of the Company in Philadelphia.

HENRY S. DURAND,

General Adjuster for the Home Insurance Company of New York.

Henry S. Durand was born February 13th, 1817, at Cheshire, New Haven County, Conn. When he was six years of age his father's family removed to Berlin, Conn., where he worked on a farm and attended the Common Schools until he was thirteen years of age, when he entered a store in Hartford, Conn., as a clerk. In the spring of 1843 he removed to Racine, Wis., and there engaged in mercantile business, taking up the Insurance business in the spring of 1844. In 1861 he opened an office in Milwaukee, and has been continuously in the Insurance business for nearly fifty-two years. He has been connected with the Home Insurance Company of New York for forty years, and has been its General Adjuster and Attorney for the sixteen Northwestern and Southwestern States for the last thirty-seven years, and is still in that service. Mr. Durand was married in 1838 to Miss Caroline B. Cowles, of Meriden, Conn. His second wife was Miss Gertrude Marion Whipple, of Pittsfield, Mass. His present wife is a daughter of Dr. Vassal White, of Stockbridge, Mass. Mr. Durand has three living daughters by his first wife, all of whom are graduates of Vassar College, and they have also received a thorough musical education. Mr. Durand made Racine, Wis., his home for forty-seven years, but his headquarters have been in Chicago since 1867. He removed to Chicago where he now resides in 1890. Mr. Durand has been a member of the Congregational church for the last sixty-seven years, and has always been a stanch Republican. He has made the reading of law a specialty for sixty years, and particularly the law of Insurance, but declares that he is still a learner.

GEORGE G. EBBERT,

Special Agent, Scottish Union and National Insurance Company.

Mr. Ebbert was born in Chicago, Ill., July 31, 1863, and obtained his education in the Chicago Public Schools. His early business training was received in one of Chicago's wholesale hardware houses. Mr. Ebbert has been in the Insurance business about ten years. Early in the year of 1887 he entered the office of the Western Department of the Connecticut Fire Insurance Company, at Chicago, and July, 1892, he went with Munger, Ebbert & Co., supervising the outside business for companies represented by them in Cook County and vicinity.

April, 26, 1891, Mr. Ebbert was married to Miss Emma L. Smith, of Chicago, and has one child. He is a member of several secret and social organizations. His father, who is still living, was the first engineer to run a locomotive out of Chicago.

GEORGE MANTON EDDY,

Special Agent and Adjuster of the Pennsylvania Fire Insurance Company.

George Manton Eddy was born in New York City on the 26th of September, 1870, and received a Common School education in Boston and Chicago. September, 1885, he entered the Insurance business as filing clerk in the office of the Commercial Union Assurance Company, Western Department, advanced to the position of Chief Examiner in 1890, resigning January 1st, 1895, to become Special Agent and Adjuster for the Pennsylvania Fire, in Northern Illinois and Indiana.

Mr. Eddy is a son of H. C. Eddy, Resident Secretary of the Commercial Union.

He was married at Chicago, Ill., in 1891, to Miss Martha B. Sprague and has two children, both boys. He is a member of the Illinois State Board and Indiana Association of Fire Underwriters.

HARRISON F. ESPENCHEID,

Special Agent of the National Insurance Company of Hartford, Conn.

Harrison F. Espenscheid was born at St. Louis, Missouri, November 5th, 1872; was educated in the Public Schools and the Washington University of St. Louis, Mo. In June, 1887, he entered the insurance business in his father's office at Sedalia, Missouri. He left Sedalia on the 1st of May, 1893, and entered the employ of the National Insurance Company, as clerk in the general office, and in August, 1893, was appointed Special Agent.

CARL EUGENE FAYE,

Special Agent, Orient Insurance Company of Hartford, Conn.

Carl Eugene Faye was born at Christiania, Norway, on the 6th of February, 1858. At the age of seventeen he graduated from a private school in Christiania and entered the office of a Wholesale Lumber Merchant and Shipowner as an apprentice; remained there two years and then went to Scotland, France and Germany to complete his education. Returning to Norway, he became clerk in a bank. After three years he resigned, came to America and located at Chicago, where he worked for a year and a half for the firm of Packer, McDonald & Bliss, Wholesale Hats and Caps, both in the stock and as traveling salesman, and was later employed by S. E. Gross & Co. as salesman until he started in business for himself. He entered the Insurance business at Parkside, Illinois, some time in 1888.

Mr. Faye is Arenon of Amity Council, No. 13 Royal League. He was married in 1887, to Miss Dagmar Olsen, and has two boys, Leslie E., six years old, and Thomas S., one year old.

ERASMUS P. FOREMAN,

Special Agent, of the Franklin Fire Insurance Company of Philadelphia, Pa.

Erasmus P. Foreman was born at Guys Mills, Crawford County, Penn., March 5th, 1836. He received his education in the Public Schools and Academy at Randolph, New York, and at the age of eighteen years was appointed a Deputy under his father, who was then Sheriff of Warren County, Penn. A year later he entered a country store and continued in the mercantile business until 1865 in connection with which from 1863 he conducted a Local Insurance business, representing the Aetna, Niagara and other companies. In 1866 he was engaged as Special Agent of the Home Insurance of New Haven for the States of Michigan, Ohio and Indiana, his field being subsequently changed to include Ohio, Kentucky and Tennessee, with headquarters at Cincinnati, with which company he remained until 1870, resigning to enter the service of the Lamar of Chicago, which company failed the following year, and for the next six months Mr. Foreman was connected with the Andes, Amazon and Triumph, placing agencies in New England. He resigned this position in 1872 and engaged with the Connecticut Fire, with which company he remained until April, 1873, when he entered the service of the Franklin Fire Insurance Company as Special Agent for the States of Michigan, Indiana and Ohio, making his headquarters at Cleveland. Subsequently he removed to Toledo, where he remained for two years, after which his headquarters were in Detroit for five years, his field then being Michigan and Ohio. In 1884 the company changed his field, placing under his supervision the States of Michigan, Illinois, Wisconsin and Minnesota, and since that time his headquarters have been in Chicago.

Mr. Foreman was one of the original fifteen that met in Dayton, Ohio, and organized the first State Board, the foundation of the present Underwriters' Association of the Northwest. He was also a member of, and served on the first committee sent out by the National Board in 1867, to rate the towns in Michigan. Besides having been a member of the original Ohio State Board, he has also been a member of the Michigan State Board from its inception, and is now a member of the Illinois State Board. He is also a member of the Masonic Order, the Odd Fellows, United Workmen and Royal Arcanum.

Mr. Foreman was married to Miss Smith in 1864, who died two years later. He was again married in 1870 to Miss London, who died some years later, leaving one daughter. In 1877 he was married again to Mrs. Belden, by whom he has living two daughters and one son.

(131)

WILLIAM CHILDS FOWLER,

State Agent of the German-American Insurance Company of New York.

William Childs Fowler was born on the 11th of April, 1861, at San Francisco, California, receiving his education in Oakland, Cal., and in Cleveland, Ohio. His grandfather, W. H. Childs, was General Agent for Western Canada, for the Aetna Insurance Company, until his death, his father being Pacific Coast Manager for the Aetna, Hartford and Home in the early sixties. In 1876 he entered the Insurance business at Niagara Falls, New York, with his grandfather, after which he spent three years at local work in Bradford, Pa., followed by a short connection with an Agency at Buffalo, N. Y., which he severed to identify himself with the Insurance office of Moore & Janes at Chicago, Illinois. He left Moore & Janes to accept a position in the General Agency office of the Springfield Fire and Marine Insurance Company, where he remained until offered the desk of Chief Examiner in the Western Department of the German-American Insurance Company, and is now Michigan State Agent for that company.

In 1887 he was married to Miss Lucy Glover Tucker, of Louisville, Kentucky, and has one child.

WILLIAM FLETCHER FOX,

Secretary of the Local Board Commissions.

William Fletcher Fox was born at Lima, LaGrange County, Ind., August 13th, 1836, of North Irish parentage. He was raised on a farm and did farm work summers and taught school winters. His finishing education was received at the University of Wisconsin. He afterwards read law and was admitted to the bar in November, 1857, practicing his profession until July, 1865, when he went into insurance at Chicago. The following year he had a Local Insurance Agency at Springfield, Ill., representing a number of leading companies, including the Mutual Life of New York. He was State and Local Agent at Cleveland, Ohio, of the Putnam Insurance Company from 1868 to 1871, then for five years Special Agent in the West and South for the Phoenix of Hartford. He returned to Chicago in 1876 as Special Agent and Adjuster. In 1881 he was appointed to his present responsible position of Secretary of the Local Board Commissioners, numbers two and three of the Western Union. Mr. Fox published in 1878 the first edition of his "Insurance Handbook," for Special Agents and Adjusters. Second and third editions have since been published.

Mr. Fox was married September 3d, 1861, to Miss Mary Dodge, of Dodgeville, Wisconsin. They have four grown children, one son and three daughters.

JOHN H. FREE,

Special Agent and Adjuster, German Insurance Company of Freeport, and Milwaukee Mechanics' Insurance Company of Milwaukee.

John H. Free was born October 29th, 1858, at Chicago, Ill. His parents located in Cook County in the town of Lyons, in 1852, coming from the State of New York. In 1855 they took up their residence in Chicago, where they have remained ever since.

Mr. Free received his education in the Public Schools, preparing himself for business by a course in Bryant & Stratton's Business College. He commenced business in 1874 with the firm of Fisher Bros., remained with them for three and a half years, then became connected with the firm of Montgomery & Talmadge as chief clerk, then with Geo. W. Montgomery and Geo. W. Montgomery & Co., remaining with them for fourteen years. In 1891 he resigned his position with the above firm, and became connected as Special Agent and Adjuster for the German Insurance Company of Freeport, and the Milwaukee Mechanics' Insurance Company of Milwaukee, Wis., under the management of Simeon Schupp, who died in 1893 and was succeeded by W. E. Spangenberg.

Mr. Free is a member of the Garden City Lodge, No. 145, K. of P.; Unity Council, No. 16, Royal League; Underwriters' Council National Union. He was married November 15th, 1883, to Miss Hattie May Van Slyke, of Fort Plain, N. Y.

CHARLES ROLAND GADSDEN,

Adjuster.

Charles Roland Gadsden was born on the 12th of December, 1859, at Dyersville, Iowa. He was educated at St. Mary's College, Dayton, Ohio, afterward studying several years in Frankfort-on-the-Main, Heidelberg and Strasburg, Germany. Since completing his education, he has been almost constantly in the Insurance business, excepting one year, 1878, when he was employed in a wholesale dry goods house, and one season, 1882-3, which he spent as a theatrical manager.

Mr. Gadsden was married at Albany, New York, November 30th, 1882, to Miss Mary Louise Newton, and has a little girl, seven years old.

DAVID L. GARDINER,

Special Agent of the Union Assurance Society of London.

David L. Gardiner was born at Abroath, Scotland, June 4th, 1867, and was educateo in the Abroath Public Schools. He entered the service of the Caledonian Railroad Company of Scotland, as a clerk, in 1883, and left Scotland in 1887, going directly to Aurora, Ill., where he entered the employ of the C., B. & Q. R. R. Mr. Gardiner resigned his position with the railroad company in 1890 to go into the local insurance business, and in 1891 he was appointed Special Agent of the Grand Rapids Fire Insurance Company for Illinois. In 1892, Mr. Gardiner was appointed Special Agent for the Sun Insurance office and the Union Assurance Society for Cook County under H. J. Straight & Co., and in 1893 he was appointed Special Agent in the West for the Union of London, which position he now holds.

Mr. Gardiner married Miss Jennie B. Drew of Aurora, Ill., on the 19th of June, 1890, and has two children, a boy and a girl. He is President of the Cook County Fieldmen's Association, and a member of the Knights of Pythias, and Caledonian and St. Andrew's Societies.

GEORGE CRESWELL GILL,

Special Agent, Atlas Insurance Company of London, England.

George Creswell Gill was born at Olympian Springs, Ky.; was educated mainly by a private teacher and at intervals attended the Public Schools of his State and finished his education at Fairview Seminary, Bath County, Ky. He was raised on a farm and entered business in a general country store at the age of fourteen, where he remained until 1876, becoming connected with the Insurance business in January, 1864, at Camargo, Illinois, while a merchant and station and express agent. Was Special Agent of the Aetna Insurance Company from 1882 to 1888, inclusive; then State Agent of the Traders', and the American of Philadelphia; then with the Atlas of England for Illinois, Michigan, Ohio, Indiana, Kentucky and Tennessee.

Mr. Gill was married in May, 1866, to Miss Jennie A. Bright at Tuscola, Illinois, and has five children—three boys and two girls, all living. He is a Knight Templar and connected with various Masonic fraternities and a member of the Iroquois Club. He was elected President of the Illinois State Board of Fire Underwriters in 1891.

GEORGE W. GILL,

Inspector and Surveyor, Phenix Insurance Company of New York.

George Washington Gill was born at Brooklyn, New York, in October, 1856. He was educated in England at the Ongar Grammar School and in 1881 entered the Insurance business and for eleven years was an Insurance Map Surveyor.

Mr. Gill was married at Zanesville, Ohio, in 1882, to Miss L. Blandy Parkhurst.

H. H. GLIDDEN,

Manager, Chicago Underwriters' Association.

In July, 1875, Mr. Glidden became a Local Agent at Springfield, Ill., remaining so until August, 1881. From January, 1882, to January, 1888, he was Special Agent for the North British and Mercantile Insurance Company. In January, 1888, he was appointed Assistant Superintendent of the Western Department of the same company, and Resident Secretary of the Chicago Branch, in August, 1889, remaining so until August, 1894, since which time he has been Manager of the Chicago Underwriters' Association.

WILLIAM E. GOLDEN,

Special Agent, Grand Rapids Insurance Company of Michigan.

William E. Golden was born in Manchester, England, on the 15th of November, 1858. He received his education in the American Public Schools, completing with a course at St. Charles College, Maryland.

In 1879 he entered the Insurance business in New York City. He was married April 7th 1891, at Grand Rapids, Michigan, to Miss Clara L. Wellenstein.

T. C. GOODMAN,

Editor of the Bulletin, Western Underwriters'.Union.

Thomas Chard Goodman, who was born at Canton, Ohio, September 7th, 1854, is the youngest son of Thomas Goodman. He has lived in Chicago since 1861, and has been Editor of the Bulletin for sixteen years.

Mr. Goodman was married September 11th, 1877, to Miss Jeanette M. Wampler, of Mankato, Minn., and has twin daughters.

J. H. GRAY,

Special Agent, North British and Mercantile Insurance Company.

J. H. Gray was born in Chicago, Illinois, Nov. 11th, 1868, and was educated in the Common Schools of his native city.

The first business he engaged in was Insurance, which he entered in September, 1877, with the Chicago Board of Underwriters, resigning to accept a position with the British America Assurance Company of Toronto, Canada, under F. Van Voorhis, Manager. In 1882, he entered the office of T. S. Cunningham & Co.; was with the Connecticut of Hartford in 1886, being appointed Special Agent of the Connecticut for Cook County, June 1st, 1893, and accepting his present position with the North British and Mercantile, January 1st, 1895.

Mr. Gray was married August 1st, 1892, to Miss Martha Gilbert, and has one child, a boy. He is a member of the Underwriters' Council, No. 258, National Union, and is Vice-President for the present term.

(142)

CECIL ALLEN HALL,

Special Agent. United Firemen's Insurance Company of Philadelphia.

Cecil Allen Hall was born in Milo, Yates County, New York, June 24th, 1844. Two years later his parents moved to Monroe County, Michigan, and in 1849 located in Toledo, Ohio, where young Cecil received his education.

In 1859 he entered the employ of the Michigan Southern & Northern Indiana Railroad, and after a year's service engaged with the firm of Bond & Messinger, wholesale boot and shoe dealers of Toledo, O. During the war he was a private in "H" Battery, First Ohio Light Artillery, and was in the Army of the Potomac. In 1865 he again associated himself with Bond & Messinger, traveling for them through Ohio and Indiana until 1867, when he entered into the manufacturing business with his uncle, Mr. C. W. Hall, continuing with him until 1875, when he and Mr. Wilson established the firm of Hall & Wilson, as local agents of the "Orient," at Toledo. In 1879 Mr. Hall was assistant secretary of the local board at Toledo, O., and in 1881 he was elected Secretary of the local board at Springfield, O.; in 1883 he was manager of the Michigan Central Compact at Kalamazoo, Mich., and in 1884 was appointed to his present position.

In November, 1869, Mr. Hall was married to Miss Nettie Hoag, who died two years later, and in 1875 he married Miss Addie L. Ketcham.

He is a charter member of the Forsyth Post, No. 15, G. A. R., of Toledo, O.; also a member of the Toledo Council, No. 21, Royal Arcanum.

JEROME B. HALL,

Special Agent and Adjuster, Girard Insurance Company of Philadelphia.

Jerome B. Hall was born in Chemung County, New York, February 22d, 1835, and was educated at Dickinson Seminary, Penn. He came West in 1862, and entered the Insurance business as solicitor, in 1863. He was married in 1871, at Rockford, Illinois, to Miss Clara E. Stratton.

On the 11th day of October, 1871, he accepted the position which he now occupies.

HENRY HALL,

Special Agent for Chicago and Cook County of the German-American
Insurance Company of New York

Henry Hall was born at Leeds, England, February 11th, 1858, receiving his education in the Common Schools of England. When twelve years of age he entered a law office as clerk; after which he pursued mechanical engineering for some time and then was apprenticed to a sailing vessel in the Allan Royal Mail Line. A sea life was not to his taste, however, and he ran away at Montreal and came to Chicago in August, 1873, when fifteen years of age, since which time he has been engaged in various pursuits. In 1882 he enlisted in the United States Cavalry, and served in various forts on the plains until 1887. In December of that year he entered the employ of the German-American Insurance Company as clerk in the Western Department.

Mr. Hall's father was a Unitarian clergyman at Leeds. Eng., and his brother, Charles, is Special Agent for the German-American Insurance Company for the State of Wisconsin.

(145)

JOSEPH HAINSWORTH,

State Agent, Milwaukee Mechanics Insurance Company of Wisconsin, for Illinois and Indiana.

Joseph Hainsworth was born in England in 1843. He came with his parents to America ten years afterwards, locating at Providence, R. I., where he worked in the cotton mills until removing to Milwaukee in 1857. Here he attended the public schools until 1861, when he entered the employ of Allis & McGregor, Bankers and Insurance Agents.

In 1862 Mr. Hainsworth removed to La Crosse, Wis., and took the position of teller in the Batavian Bank, and in 1864 was cashier of the Columbia Bank at Portage, Wis., where he also represented a good line of Insurance Companies. Removing to Chicago in 1871 in time to see his savings go up in the great fire, he entered the General office of the Hartford Fire Insurance Company. In the fall of 1881 Mr. Hainsworth associated himself with the Northwestern National Insurance Company as Special Agent for Illinois and Iowa, resigning in 1894 to take the position of State Agent of the Milwaukee Mechanics'. He was married February, 1866, at Portage, Wisconsin, to Miss J. Kate Miller.

JOHN HANRAHAN,

Special Agent. Liverpool & London & Globe Insurance Company.

Mr. Hanrahan entered the Insurance business in the office of Messrs. Moore & Janes, of this city, in April, 1883, since which time he has followed his chosen calling. Entering the service of the Liverpool & London & Globe Insurance Company in August, 1887, his first service was as a clerk, and he has reached his present position of Special Agent through well-deserved promotion. Mr. Hanrahan is still a young man, having been born in Green Bay, Wis., December 26th, 1859, and his Insurance knowledge is supplemented by his education, received in the public schools of the city of his birth.

RICHARD D. HARVEY,

Special Agent, Greenwich Insurance Company of New York.

Richard D. Harvey was born at Arcola, Ill., September 25th, 1858, and was educated in the Public Schools of that place. After leaving school, he was employed as clerk in a general store until 1878, when he emigrated to Nebraska, locating at Republican City, embarking in the drug and grocery business, remaining there until 1880, when he located at Springfield, Mo., and became a local Fire insurance Agent there, continuing that until 1882, when he was appointed Special Agent for the German Insurance Company of Peoria, Ill., which position he held until 1888, when he was made General Agent at Chicago for the People's Fire Insurance Company of Manchester, N. H., continuing as such until the failure of the Company in October, 1893; he was then engaged by the Greenwich Insurance Company for the position he holds at present as Special Agent.

Mr. Harvey was married October 12th, 1887, at Danville, Ill., to Miss Luella B. Tincher.

GEORGE WASHBURN HAYES,

Illinois Special Agent, Lancashire Insurance Company of Manchester, England.

George Washburn Hayes was born at Waverly, Illinois, May 25th, 1864. October 13th of that year his father, George Warren Hayes, now of Milwaukee, Wisconsin, Manager of the Northwestern Department of the Western, and British America Assurance Companies of Toronto, Canada, was appointed Local Agent of the Aetna Insurance Company at Waverly, Illinois, by C. C. Hine, then Special Agent, under General Agent J. B. Bennett, now editor of the Insurance Monitor of New York City; so "George Jr.," was brought up in the Insurance fold.

His experience in the Local Agency work was gained in the employ of Callendar & Co., Peoria, Ill.; Weed & Lawrence, St. Paul, Minn., and Judge E. B. Ames of Minneapolis, Minn. The first Insurance work done by him as Special Agent was the appointment of an agent of the Western Assurance Company, whose commission bears the date of March 14th, 1882.

In the fall of 1891, he branched off into newspaper work, serving as Washington correspondent for the St. Paul, Minn., Daily Globe, during the first session of the Fifty-second Congress.

In May, 1892, he was appointed to the position which he still occupies, as Special Agent in Illinois, for the Lancashire. He is a member of the Executive Committee of the State Board of that State. His report upon the Fire Hazard of Electricity, made to that body last year, was his most notable work since leaving journalism.

The photograph album formerly owned by J. B. Bennett, and at his death presented to the Fire Underwriters' Association of the Northwest, contains a picture of Mr. Hayes, Jr., taken when a child, and it is noteworthy that from passing the programs as a lad during his father's seven-year term as Secretary of the association, to membership in 1892, he has missed but few meetings, and thereby become one of the best known members of the second generation of fire insurance men in the West.

HENRY HARRISON HEAFORD,

General Adjuster, Phoenix Insurance Company of Hartford, Conn.

Henry Harrison Heaford was born at Albany, New York, of English parents, on the 12th of October, 1848. He was educated in the Public Schools of Brooklyn, N. Y., and Covington, Ky., and commenced his business career in 1862 as clerk in the office of James Ayars, then Local Agent at Covington, Ky., for the Phoenix Insurance Company of Hartford, and after a preparatory course in the Western and Southern Branch Offices at Cincinnati, O., he was, in the spring of 1874, made Special Agent and Adjuster of the Phoenix for Michigan and Indiana, with headquarters at Jackson, and in May, 1883, was transferred by General Agent H. M. Magill, of said Company, to Chicago to act as General Adjuster, a position he still occupies.

August 26th, 1872, Mr. Heaford married Miss Emma V. Yates at Covington, Ky., and has had four children, two of whom are living.

LESLIE EGBERT HILDRETH,

Superintendent of Agencies for Illinois of the Hartford Fire Insurance
Company.

PERRY J. HOBBS,

General Adjuster, Hartford Fire Insurance Company.

Perry J. Hobbs was born at Ottawa, Ill., June 22d, 1848, receiving his education in the public schools of Joliet, Ill.

In 1865 he entered the Insurance business as office boy for P. C. Royce, Local Agent at Joliet (now Secretary of the Hartford Fire Insurance Company). Mr. Hobbs succeeded Mr. Royce in the local business, and has been identified with Insurance continuously since.

He was married on the anniversary of the Chicago fire, October 9th, 1872, to Miss Sarah A. Baker, of Willoughby, Ohio, and has two sons and one daughter. He is a member of the Union League Club of Chicago.

JAMES L. HOLDEN,

General Insurance Adjuster.

James L. Holden was born on the 10th day of June, 1832, at Charlestown, N. H. Richard, John and Justinian Holden emigrated from Ipswich, England, in 1642, and he is a descendant, in the eighth generation, of Richard, who lived in Groton, Mass. His great-grandfather Richard, and grandfather Timothy, were held as prisoners of war, on board prison ship in Boston Harbor, by the British during the Revolution; they were subsequently exchanged and Captain Richard was killed in battle in New Jersey.

Mr. Holden was educated at Kimball Union Academy, Meriden, N. H., after which he spent several years in a general country store; later he became a mechanical engineer, being employed for several years in a large locomotive and car shop. In 1865 he entered the Insurance business at Aurora, Illinois, as a Local Agent. Three years later he was appointed General Agent of the Equitable Life Assurance Society; then for thirteen years was State Agent of Illinois for the Insurance Company of North America.

For the past six years he has made a specialty of adjusting losses on railway property, serving the Syndicate Companies in all portions of the United States.

In 1856 Mr. Holden was married to Miss Sara Allen at Honeoye Falls, N. Y. They have had five children, three of which are now living.

JOHN HOWLEY,

Fire Insurance Adjuster.

John Howley was born at Montreal, Canada, February 16th, 1846. His earliest vocation was that of bookkeeping in a large boot and shoe store. In 1865 he came West, and in Chicago was a clerk in a wholesale millinery establishment one year before his acquaintance with fire insurance began in the local agency office of Hubbard & Hunt. In 1870 he was Secretary of the Lumbermen's Insurance Company of Chicago; in 1874 he went into the field as Special Agent for the Home of New York, and subsequently, in 1881, for the Niagara Fire. In 1883 he was appointed Western General Agent of the Scottish Union and National. In 1889 he was President of the Fire Underwriters' Association of the Northwest. He was Adjuster for the Mutual Fire of New York when President Armstrong sold the business of that Company to the Lancashire, and was transferred with it to the English Company. When Mr. Howley's contract with the Lancashire expired, May 1st, 1894, he renewed his engagement with the Mutual Fire.

ROBERT H. HUNTER,

Special Agent, Norwich Union Fire Insurance Society of England.

Robert H. Hunter is of Scotch descent, and was born in Chicago, Illinois, July 29th, 1869. He received a thorough education in the public schools of Chicago, after completing which he entered business as a clerk in the wholesale drug house of Lord, Owen & Co., where he was employed from 1885 to 1889, resigning to enter the insurance business with the firm of D. S. Munger & Co., and later being appointed Special Agent of the Norwich Union Fire Insurance Society.

He is a member of Dearborn Lodge, No. 310, F. & A. M., La Fayette Chapter No. 1, and Apollo Commandery No. 1, K. T.

ROBERT JARDINE,

Chief Inspector, Improved Risks Commission.

Robert Jardine was born at Dumbarton, Scotland, January 22d, 1852. He received his education in the parochial schools at Helensburgh, Dumbartonshire. Between the ages of fourteen and sixteen he filled the position of an assistant bookkeeper, but preferring the more independent occupation of a mechanic, he apprenticed himself to a house painter and decorator. His mother dying in the early part of 1871, he with his sister emigrated to this country, settling in Ohio, September 1st, 1871. Finding his trade in poor condition, he joined his brothers, who were in business at that point, and learned the plumbing and steam-fitting trades. In 1885 he engaged himself to a Cincinnati heating and ventilating house as constructing engineer; staying there but a few months, being offered a position as contracting agent for the Western Department of the Providence Steam and Gas Pipe Company, to sell the Grinnell system of automatic sprinklers, which he accepted early in 1886. In 1889 he accepted a position as inspector with two mutual companies then being organized at Winona, Minn., by the lumbermen of the Northwest; remaining with these companies two years he was called upon to assume the management of the new Western Department for the Neracher & Hill Sprinkler Company. The department was hardly in working order when an offer of his present position was tendered him by the late E. A. Simonds, Chairman of the Committee on Improved Risks, which position he still continues to fill.

In 1877, at Springfield, Ohio, he married Miss Mary Louise Voll; three children, all living, have blessed their union. Mr. Jardine belongs to the Masonic and Knights of Pythias Societies and is a member of the Caledonian Society of this city.

JAMES J. JOHNSON,

Special Agent and Adjuster, Niagara Fire Insurance Company.

James J. Johnson was born at Chicago, Illinois, September 13th, 1863, and received his education in the grammar schools of that city.

August 1st, 1880, he entered the employ of the Niagara Fire Insurance Company at Chicago, and after a service of fourteen years in the Western Department office, a large portion of which time as Chief Examiner of Daily Reports, he was appointed Special Agent and Adjuster for Illinois.

He is a member of Cleveland Lodge, No. 211, A. F. and A. M.; Prairie State Council, No. 912, Royal Arcanum; Schiller Council, No. 23, and Royal League.

HORATIO N. KELSEY,

State Agent and Adjuster, Norwich Union Fire Insurance Society of England.

Horatio Nelson Kelsey first engaged in the Insurance business in the year 1886, entering a local agency in Indianapolis. In 1888 he came to Chicago in the employ of Charles Lyman Case, Manager of the London Assurance Corporation, serving in the capacity of Special Agent for Iowa, Missouri, Kansas and Nebraska. In 1890 he accepted the position he now holds with the Norwich Union.

Mr. Kelsey is a member of the Chicago Athletic Association, and the Sigma Chi Greek College Fraternity.

EDWARD D. KINNEY,

**Assistant General Agent of Cook County for the American Central Insurance
Company and New Hampshire Fire Insurance Company.**

Edward D. Kinney was born in New York State, and has been in the Insurance business
for about twenty years. He married Miss Mary E. Faust, and has one daughter.

JOHN W. KINNEY,

General Adjuster, Agricultural Insurance Company.

John W. Kinney was born at Madison, New York, on the 16th of June, 1838, and entered the Insurance business in 1868.

N. A. LAUER,

Special Agent. Hanover Insurance Company, New York.

Nicholas A. Lauer was born in Chicago (Fort Dearborn), January 19th, 1851. He is one of the few now alive who were born in old Fort Dearborn. His father, who was killed September 17th, 1854, was one of the first police officers killed in the discharge of his duty in Chicago.

After completing his education in St. Xavier's College, Cincinnati, Ohio, he entered into the Abstract business with Chase Bros., Chicago, remaining with them for eight years. He was afterwards a clerk in the office of the Superior Court of Cook County and in 1878 entered the Insurance business as a broker at Chicago.

Mr. Lauer was married in Chicago to Miss Elizabeth P. Rees, whose parents were among the oldest settlers in the city, moving here in 1833.

(161)

CHARLES W. LEISCH,

Special Agent, Michigan Fire and Marine Insurance Company of Detroit, Mich.

Chas. W. Leisch was born in 1858, at Peshtigo, Wisconsin. He received his primary education in a Parochial School at Green Bay, Wis., preparing himself for his business life by a course in a business college at the same place. He began business in 1871, as clerk in a crockery store, and at the expiration of a few months went to work as office boy in a local insurance office at Green Bay, Wis., where he remained until 1879, when he came to Chicago and entered the office of the Phenix of Brooklyn as clerk. Later he was employed by the Firemans' Fund Insurance Company, resigning in 1882 to engage with the Phoenix of England, and in January, 1888, was appointed to a field position for the company, which position he held until 1889, when he became connected with the Anglo-Nevada, remaining with that Company until it re-insured in the Caledonian, and in January, 1892, changed to the Michigan F. and M. Insurance Company, with which he is still connected.

He was married at Chicago in 1884, to Miss Lizzie M. Meyers; has one child, a boy.

J. H. LENEHAN,

Special Agent, Palatine Insurance Company of England.

J. H. Lenehan was born at Dubuque, Iowa. Previous to engaging with his present company, the Palatine, he was State Agent in Illinois for the Insurance Company of North America and the Pennsylvania Fire.

May 9th, 1883, he was married to Margaret Littleton, daughter of Henry A. Littleton, formerly of Memphis, Tenn., who was one of the most prominent Insurance Agents in the South.

GEO. M. LOVEJOY,

Special Agent, German American Insurance Company, of New York.

Geo. M. Lovejoy was born on the eleventh day of August, 1857, in Waterville, Maine. He received his primary education at the Westbrook Seminary of Maine and Phillips Academy of Andover, Massachusetts, and was graduated from Tufts College of Massachusetts in 1882. His first business venture was as a clerk in a boot and shoe store, after which he taught school. In 1883 he entered the insurance business at Chicago with the German American Insurance Co., of New York. September 15, 1886, he was married to Ellen M. Whitcomb at Littleton, Massachusetts; they had two children, one of whom is living. Mr. Lovejoy is a member of the "Theta Delta Chi" Fraternity, Sons and Daughters of Maine of Chicago, Chicago Athletic Association, and the Fire Underwriters' Association of the Northwest, of which he was elected president, September 15, 1895.

FREDERICK BARCLAY LUCE

Special Agent of the Palatine Insurance Company.

Frederick Barclay Luce was born at Alpena, Michigan, and was educated in the public schools of Detroit, Michigan. In March, 1892, he entered the General Agency office of the Phoenix Insurance Company, of Brooklyn, N. Y. He was with that Company for seven months, leaving it to take a position with the Western Factory Association, which he held until September, 1894, resigning them to take his present position with the Palatine Insurance Company, Ltd.

WILLIAM ALLISON LYON,

Special Agent, National Fire Insurance Company, Hartford, Conn., for Illinois and Indiana.

William Allison Lyon is a native of Aberdeen, Scotland, where he was born on the 8th day of January, 1840. He arrived in this country at an early age and settled in Jefferson County, Indiana, where he received his primary education, and later entered a commercial college at Cincinnati, Ohio, after which he became a farmer and school teacher until 1861, when he enlisted in the Sixth Regiment, Indiana Volunteers, and served in that regiment three years. He was severely wounded at the battle of Chickamauga, but recovered and re-enlisted in the Fifth Regiment, United States Veteran Volunteers, and served until the close of the war.

Mr. Lyon then engaged in the mercantile pursuits until 1871, when he entered the Insurance business with the Franklin Insurance Company of Indianapolis, remaining with that Company until 1886, when he came to Chicago as Special Agent of the Washington Fire and Marine Insurance Company of Boston, and two years later, when that Company re-insured in the National, he was appointed to his present position by General Agent F. S. James.

L. A. Moore entered the Insurance business in the office of the Royal Insurance Company in June, 1885.

ROBERT R. MANNERS,

Special Adjuster, Phenix Insurance Company of Brooklyn. N. Y.

Robert R. Manners was born of English parents, at Granby, near Newcastle, Ontario, Canada, in October, 1850. In 1871, Mr. Manners entered the employ of the Ontario Government, in the Department of Public Instruction, where he remained sufficiently long to discover that the advancement under the regulations of government civil service was not likely to keep pace with his ambition. Accordingly he tendered his resignation in the spring of 1872 and removed to New York. In May of that year he entered the service of the Erie Railway Company, as private secretary to the president. In this employ he remained for about two years, having part of that time acted in the same capacity to the chief of the passenger department, John M. Abbott.

It was in September, 1874, that he connected himself with fire underwriting by entering the employ of the Continental Fire of New York, in whose service he remained for nearly ten years.

December, 1883, two opportunities were offered him to engage in field work; One with the National Fire of Hartford, for the States of New York and Pennsylvania; and the other with the Northwestern Department of the Royal, and London & Lancashire Insurance Companies, under the management of C. H. Case. This latter position was accepted, and in January, 1884, Mr. Manners removed to Chicago and took charge of the State of Michigan for the companies named, with Northern Illinois, and later, Wisconsin, as an additional territory. This field he managed with recognized skill and success, making an exceptional record, more particularly in the difficult State of Michigan. After four years' service with the Royal, he, in January, 1888, accepted the position of Adjuster in the field at large with the Western Department of the Phenix of New York. He now holds the position of Special Adjuster with that company with whom he has long enjoyed an enviable reputation.

Mr. Manners occupies a prominent position in his profession and is a man of recognized business ability and literary attainments; a genial companion and an accomplished gentleman.

W. E. MARINER,

Special Agent, American Insurance Company of Newark, N. J.

W. E. Mariner was born April 1st, 1867, at Independence, Missouri; received his education in Public Schools and private academies of that locality, and began the fire Insurance business as a Local Agent at Olathe, Kansas, in 1885. In 1887 he became Special Agent in Missouri and Kansas for an Iowa Company, and in 1889 became Home Office Adjuster for the Standard Fire Insurance Company, at Kansas City, Missouri. In 1891, Mr. Mariner became Special Agent for the American Insurance Company, of Newark, New Jersey, and is at present connected with that Company as their Western Special Agent, having charge of Indiana, Illinois, Michigan, Minnesota, Wisconsin, Missouri, Kansas, Nebraska, Iowa and Indian Territory. He was married December 11th, 1885, at St. Louis, Mo., to Miss Sada F. McMillin, and has two children.

I. F. MARSHALL,

Independent Adjuster.

J. F. Marshall was born in Chicago, April, 1841, receiving his education in the public schools. He started in the insurance business in 1865 as a solicitor for E. E. Ryan & Co. From the time of the Chicago fire in 1871 until the summer of 1872 he was located in the Home office in Cincinnati, of the Andes, Amazon and Triumph Insurance Companies, having supervision of the Abstract Department of these companies. In January, 1873, he became connected with the Lycoming Insurance Company as Special Agent and Adjuster for the Northwest, and remained with that company until 1881. In the spring of 1881 he entered the service of Straight & Lyman, as Special Agent and Adjuster for the New York Alliance, composed of the Pacific and Bowery Insurance Companies. He remained with this company until 1883, when he resigned his position to enter the field as an Independent Adjuster, and was commissioned to take up the agencies of the Star Insurance Company of New York and several of the agencies of the Union Insurance company of Philadelphia in the West and Southwest.

Mr. Marshall's father was in the insurance business in 1865, running a Local Agency for some years. He was one of the earliest settlers in Chicago at the time of his death, which occurred in March, 1891, at the age of eighty-two, holding the Gold Medal for being the oldest settler.

In August, 1871, Mr. Marshall was married, losing his estimable wife by death in April 1881. He is a member of the Knights of Pythias, and Past Grand Chancellor of Banner Lodge, No. 219, K. of P.

J. J. McCARTHY,

Special Agent for Cook County of the Caledonian Insurance Company, Spring
Garden Insurance Company of Philadelphia, and the Insurance
Company of the State of Pennsylvania.

John J. McCarthy was born at Chicago, Illinois, September 19th, 1868, received his
primary education in the public schools of that city and spent two years in college. October 24th, 1885, he entered the Insurance office of R. S. Critchell & Co., at Chicago, Ill., with
which firm he is still connected.

He was married in Chicago, to Miss Marion L. Conway; they have one child, a girl.

Mr. McCarthy is a member of the Columbus Club of Chicago.

LOUIS SHIRLEY McMILLAN,
Adjuster of Fire Losses.

Louis Shirley McMillan was born in Chicago, October 28th, 1855. He received his education in public and private schools of his native city and of Piqua and Columbus, Ohio, and Wheeling, West Virginia, and at the National Business College in the latter city, after which, on August 17th, 1870, he entered the employ of John Roemer & Co., dry goods merchants, at Wheeling, as cashier and bookkeeper, remaining with them until November 4th, 1872, when he entered the Insurance business with the Franklin Insurance Company at their home office in Wheeling. While with the Franklin he continued keeping the books of his former employers after night and until September 20th, 1875, when he moved to St. Louis, Missouri. From October, 1875, to March 26th, 1879, he was employed in that city by the Scottish Commercial Insurance Company, of Glasgow, Scotland, as bookkeeper, and when that Company moved its Western Department headquarters to Chicago, he moved with them and continued in their service until after the amalgamation of the "Scottish" with the Lancashire of England, or until May 24th, 1880, when he was appointed chief clerk in the Western Department office of the Star Fire Insurance Company of New York, and the Union Insurance Company of Philadelphia, which position he retained until June 1st, 1881, when he entered the employ of the Niagara Fire Insurance Company of New York as bookkeeper for the newly consolidated Western Department, under the management of I. S. Blackwelder. In 1883, Mr. McMillan was appointed Special Agent for the "Niagara" in Ohio and West Virginia, and later in the same year, was transferred to Illinois, remaining in that State as Special Agent and Adjuster until January 1st, 1892, when he was transferred to the West and became Supervising Agent and Adjuster for the "Niagara" and the Caledonian Insurance Company of Edinburgh, Scotland, for the States of Missouri, Kansas and Nebraska, and Oklahoma and Indian Territory, with headquarters at Kansas City, Missouri. He remained in the West until January 1st, 1894, when the Western Department of the "Niagara" and "Caledonian" was closed, when he returned to Chicago and has since been engaged in the adjustment of losses on his own account.

Mr. McMillan was Secretary and Treasurer of the Illinois State Board of Fire Underwriters in 1889 and 1890, and for some years a member of the Executive Committee of that body and also Chairman of important district committees. He has been a member of the Fire Underwriters' Association of the Northwest since 1883.

Mr. McMillan is the author of "Special Agents' Ten Year Comparative Record and Agency Statistics," which is published by the Rough Notes Company of Indianapolis, Indiana, and is regarded as one of the most complete and valuable field books for the use of Special Agents ever published.

(171)

F. A. MEINEL,

Special Agent London and Lancashire Fire Insurance Company.

Frank A. Meinel was born at Chicago, Illinois, August 18th, 1870, and was educated in the Public Schools. He commenced business at Chicago, September 11th, 1884, in the Western Department of the New York Alliance, under the management of E. W. Lyman, and remained until the discontinuance of its Western Department, January, 1887, then entering the Local Agency of Edward M. Teall & Co., and in April, 1888, became connected with the London and Lancashire, under Mr. J. S. Belden.

Mr. Meinel is a member of the Masonic Fraternity and Menoken Club.

E. C. MEINEL,

Special Agent. Manchester Fire Assurance Company.

E. C. Meinel was born at Chicago, Illinois, on the 28th of January, 1869, being educated in the public schools of that city. He has been connected with Insurance since the beginning of his business career, entering the employ of the Underwriters' Exchange, at Chicago, in February, 1884.

At the time the Manchester Fire Assurance Company established its United States Department at Cheiago, he became connected with them as Special Agent in various States, and is now representing them in New York in that capacity.

FRANK R. MILLARD,

General Adjuster, Western Department, Continental Insurance Company of New York.

Frank R. Millard is a native of New York State. He came West early and received his education at Clark's Seminary of Aurora, Ill., and Hillsdale College, Michigan. He then entered the employ of the American Express Company as clerk and road agent, and in May, 1870, entered the service of the Continental Insurance Company in their Chicago office. Ten years later he was appointed Special Agent for the Company in Michigan, then recalled to Chicago to fill the position of Special Adjuster for the Western Department, in which capacity he served eight years. In May, 1893, he was appointed to his present position.

Mr. Millard was married in Chicago to Miss Adaline E. Dart, and is a member of the Ashland Club.

L. A. MOORE,

Special Agent, Royal Insurance Company.

L. A. Moore entered the Insurance business in the office of the Royal Insurance Company in June, 1885.

MORRISON S. MOORE,

Special Agent, Rhode Island Underwriters' Association.

Morrison S. Moore was born in Clark County, Illinois, on the 15th of February, 1856. When he was three years old his father moved to the State of Kansas, where he received a common school education. When seventeen years of age he entered a commercial school at Ft. Scott, Kan. After completing the course he engaged as a telegraph operator for some time, entering the insurance business at Rockford, Ill., in 1878. He was married at Marshall, Ill., March 29th, 1877, to Miss Orinthia A. Pearce.

GEORGE C. MOTT,

State Agent and Adjuster of the St. Paul Fire and Marine Insurance Company.

George C. Mott was born in New York City, December 29th, 1861, and was educated in the public and private schools of St. Paul, Minn. He commenced his business career in the office of Hughson & Hemenway, Insurance Agents, at St. Paul, then went to the St. Paul Fire and Marine Insurance Company. He has been with the "St. Paul" for more than ten years, and has been in almost every department of the Home office and on the road, as State Agent for seven years.

Mr. Mott is a member of the B. P. O. Elks, No. 59, St. Paul.

G. MUELLER,

State Agent for The Merchants' Insurance Company of Newark, N. J.

G. Mueller was born in Germany, March 28th, 1867. His parents emigrated to America in the spring of 1868 and settled in Chicago, where Mr. Mueller received his education in public and private schools. January 2d, 1883, he entered the Local Agency office of G. H. Koch in Chicago. Resigning this position he entered the employ of the Western Department of the Germania Fire Insurance Company of New York, September 10th, 1885. In 1892 he was appointed Special Agent for Nebraska and Kansas, resigning December 1st, 1894, to accept his present position.

EUGENE V. MUNN,

General Adjuster, Insurance Company of North America and Philadelphia Underwriters.

Eugene V. Munn was born at Freeport, Illinois, February 10th, 1852, and was educated in the district schools of his county and the Freeport High School. After leaving school he was a clerk in his father's store, until May 9th, 1872, when he entered the office of the American Insurance Company of Chicago, at Chicago, as office boy, where he remained until 1880. From 1880 to 1889 he was State Agent for Wisconsin of the Continental Insurance Company of New York; 1887 to 1889 was President of the Wisconsin State Board of Underwriters; 1890 was Vice-President of the Fire Underwriters' Association of the Northwest; 1890 to 1895, Special Adjuster of the Home Insurance Company of New York; 1895 was General Adjuster of the Insurance Company of North America and the Philadelphia Underwriters; 1890 to 1895 was Secretary and Treasurer of the Fire Underwriters' Association of the Northwest.

Mr. Munn was married at Beloit, Wisconsin, September 5th, 1882, to Miss Mary Kendall, and has five children.

ANDREW M. NELSON,

Special Agent for Cook County of the Niagara Fire Insurance Company
of New York.

Andrew M. Nelson was born on the 25th of October, 1866, and was educated in the Chicago Public Schools, receiving his early training in Insurance business under the direction of Geo. C. Clarke. His rise in the ranks was rapid and steady, and two years before reaching his majority was Daily Report Examiner for the London Assurance Corporation, remaining with that Company a year and a half after Mr. Charles L. Case took the Western Department management of that Company. He left there to engage with the Niagara, under Mr. Blackwelder, and upon the removal of the Western Department to New York, went with the department, having charge of a section of field under title of Superintendent of the Western Department. Upon re-establishment of the Western Department he returned to Chicago to act as Chief Clerk in the office, relinquishing his position in the office to look after the Chicago and Cook County business of the company.

Mr. Nelson was married September 17th, 1890, to Miss Edith Thornberg, and has two children, a girl and boy.

(180)

ROBERT S. ODELL,

State Agent and Adjuster, Connecticut Insurance Company.

Robert S. Odell was born in Hopewell, Ontario County, N. Y., April 17th, 1850, and was educated in Canandaigua Academy. Entering the insurance business at Chicago, January 15th, 1871, he was with the Continental Insurance Company for nineteen years; with the German-American two years, and with his present company, the Connecticut Fire, for the past three years.

He was married in 1888, and is a member of the Methodist Episcopal Church, Knight Templars, and the Society of the Sons of New York in Chicago.

DEMPSTER OSTRANDER,

General Adjuster, Western Department of the Phœnix Insurance Company of Brooklyn, N. Y.

Dempster Ostrander was born in Onondaga County, New York, November 20th, 1834. At the age of seven he removed with his parents to Wisconsin, then a wilderness country. In the region of his home there were not more than half a dozen families within the limits of an ordinary modern county. Settlers multiplied rapidly, however, and by the time the boy had reached the age of ten years a school house was built, and here his early education was received. At the age of twenty he entered the Wisconsin State University at Madison, where his school work was completed. In 1865 he became connected with a manufacturing enterprise at Jefferson, Wis., and as early as 1855 he had a little experience in the Insurance business, to which he has given his chief attention for a long time. He studied law, and in 1861 was admitted to the bar at Jefferson, and although he never engaged in practice, has all his life since made insurance law a study, and is regarded as an authority by the insurance fraternity, and legal profession. He has contributed numerous valuable articles on the subject for the insurance journals, and is the author of a standard text book on the law of Fire Insurance, bearing his name. His practical experience in the field of fire insurance has been large and varied, but he is best known as the General Adjuster for the Phœnix of Brooklyn, a position which he has occupied for many years.

Mr. Ostrander is a gentleman of broad culture and fine literary tastes, which he has found leisure to gratify from time to time. His latest effort in this respect was a little volume bearing the title: "Social Growth and Stability: a Consideration of the Factors of Modern Society and Their Relation to the Character of the Coming State," recently published by S. C. Griggs & Co., of this city. Judge Ostrander, as his friends call him, resided for several years in Milwaukee, but moved to Chicago some ten years ago, where he now resides.

HORACE H. PELTON,

Special Agent, Continental Insurance Company.

Horace H. Pelton was born on a farm near Shrewsbury, Mass. When he was four years old his parents moved to Maine, and one year later to Missouri, where they both died when Mr. Pelton was seven years of age. He then lived on a farm near Sedalia, Mo., attending a country school, and subsequently spending nearly two terms in the State Normal School of Kirksville, Mo. After which he taught school, engaging in various pursuits during vacation, until 1889, when he entered the Insurance business at New Orleans with the Inter State Fire Association, and has since that time been connected with different companies, among them being the Fire Association of Texas, of Waco, Texas; was Inspector of the Underwriters' Inspection Bureau of New Orleans, and served with the Texas Survey and Rating Bureau. In 1894 he became Special Agent of the Continental Insurance Company, for Wisconsin and Northern Illinois, with headquarters at Chicago.

Mr. Pelton is a member of the Underwriters' Association of the Northwest, and also of the Knights of Pythias.

CHARES F. PERSCH,

Secretary. Illinois State Board of Fire Underwriters.

   Charles F. Persch was born at Buffalo, New York, February 7th, 1856, and was
educated in the Public Schools of that city.   In 1872 he began his insurance career with
the German Insurance Company of Buffalo.   After one year with this Company, and one
year with the Marine Bank of Buffalo, he spent two years in the Insurance office of
Smith & Davis of the same place.   He came to Chicago in May, 1877, and was employed
in the office of the Traders' Insurance Company; became connected with the Springfield
Fire and Marine Insurance Company in 1878, remaining with this Company until October, 1893.   He was elected Secretary of the Illinois State Board in February, 1894.

HARRY OTIS PHILLIPS,

Special Agent, Western Department Insurance Company of the State of Pennsylvania.

Harry Otis Phillips was born at Chippewa Falls, Wisconsin, July 31st, 1867, receiving his education in the public schools of Minneapolis and the University of Minnesota. For a year, at the beginning of his business career, he was a clerk in the office of F. H. Peavey, & Co., and in January, 1890, entered the office of the Minneapolis Inspection Bureau. He had the privilege of discipline in rating under Charles T. Rothermel while the latter was rescheduling Minneapolis.

Mr. Phillips is a member of the Phi Kappa Psi (a college fraternity) and belongs to the Underwriters' Association of the Northwest.

ISAAC P. POINIER,

Adjuster.

Isaac P. Poinier was born at Cincinnati, Ohio, on the 7th of May, 1823, and received his education in Woodward College, of that city.

In 1865 he entered the Insurance business at Chicago, Ill., in the office of the Fireman's Insurance Company, and the next year became a Special for the "City Fire Insurance Company," of Hartford, Conn. After the Chicago fire he was engaged in independent work until 1879, when he entered the field again for the Lancashire Insurance Company, of England, in their Central Department, remaining until 1886.

For the last eight years he has been in the office of Messrs. Moore & James, as Adjuster of Losses and Inspector of Business.

HENRY H. RASSWEILER,

State Agent, Insurance Company of North America and Philadelphia Underwriters.

Henry H. Rassweiler was born at Orwigsburg, Pa., April 3rd, 1842. In 1862 he entered the Northwestern College (then at Plainfield, now at Naperville, Illinois) as janitor-student, graduating in 1868, from which time until 1883 he was professor of mathematics and natural science in the same institution. From 1883 to 1888 he was President of the college. After two years of service as literary editor with the Western Publishing House, at Chicago, he entered the insurance field, in 1890, as Special Agent of the Insurance Company of North America and Pennsylvania Fire, afterwards becoming State Agent of the first-named company and the Philadelphia Underwriters, a position which he still holds.

He was married in 1868, at Cedar Falls, Iowa, to Miss Victoria Harlacher, and has two children.

GEORGE E. REDFIELD,

General Adjuster.

George E. Redfield was born at Greenfield, Saratoga County, New York, December 9th, 1832. His grandfather on his father's side was a sailor on a privateer during the Revolutionary war, and his grandfather on his mother's side was a Captain in the war of 1812 with Great Britain. His father was a clergyman of the Presbyterian Church. Mr. Redfield was educated in district schools and at Delaware Academy, at Delhi, N. Y. When sixteen years old he left school and became a clerk in the hardware store of his uncle at Phelps, New York. In 1850 went to Beloit, Wis., as clerk and bookkeeper; in 1852 became salesman in a wholesale hardware house in New York City; in 1854 commenced the hardware business, on his own account, at Beaver Dam, Wis. Became Local Agent for the Aetna, Hartford and Home Insurance Companies in 1858; commenced Special Agency work for the Home of New York about 1866 and represented that Company, the New York Underwriters, Imperial, German-American, and other Companies, until he became General Agent in 1873, first for the Atlas Insurance Company of Hartford and afterwards for the Shawmut of Boston, the National of New York and the Citizens of New York. For five years was Inspector for the Eastern District of Iowa.

Mr. Redfield was married, September 17th, 1855, at Beloit, Wis., to Miss Harriet A. Clark, and has six children.

ANSON P. REDFIELD,

President of the Union Adjustment Company.

Anson P. Redfield was born at Phelps, Ontario County, New York, on the 1st of November, 1840, and was educated in the common schools. In 1855 he left school and commenced his business career as clerk in a retail hardware store at Beaver Dam, Wisconsin. Continued in that business until 1864; then engaged in the wholesale hardware business in Milwaukee as traveling salesman, and afterwards general salesman in the store. Continued in this until 1870, when he became junior partner in the wholesale hardware business at Milwaukee, which position he held until he entered the Fire Insurance business in 1874, when he became a Special Agent at Chicago.

Mr. Redfield was married on the 6th of May, 1860, at Beaver Dam, Wisconsin, to Miss Hattie Morgan, and has two children. He is a member of the Third Presbyterian Church of Chicago and the Underwriters' Association of the Northwest.

DAVID W. REDFIELD,

Special Agent and Adjuster, Pennsylvania Fire Insurance Company of
Philadelphia.

David W. Redfield was born at Delhi, New York, on the 7th of May, 1856. His family came West in his boyhood and settled at Beaver Dam, Wisconsin, where he attended the public schools, completing his education at Wayland University. After leaving college he went to Beloit, Wis., and was for six years employed in the Beloit Iron Works, resigning in 1878 to come to Chicago and enter the Insurance office of Geo. C. Clarke & Co., where he remained for six years, being then appointed Special Agent of the London Assurance Corporation and afterwards Special and General Agent of the Boylston Insurance Company of Boston. January, 1895, he was appointed to his present position, Special Agent and Adjuster for Michigan and Wisconsin of the Pennsylvania Fire Insurance Company of Philadelphia.

Mr. Redfield was married in 1892 to Miss Mellie Wilson, and has one child. He is a Mason and a member of the Royal Arcanum.

JOHN WALTER ROBERTSON

Special Agent, London and Lancashire Insurance Company.

John Walter Robertson was born at Alexandria, Va., September 9th, 1856. He studied for a lawyer in the University of Virginia, and practiced law for some years after leaving college. He entered the Insurance business in 1878 at Sterling, Kansas, and traveled as Special Agent for the National Fire Insurance Company of Hartford from 1881 to 1887, in Illinois and Wisconsin, and has been since with the London and Lancashire for Illinois, Michigan and Wisconsin.

Mr. Robertson was married at Washington, D. C., January 13th, 1886, to Miss Carrie M. Wyville, and has one child. He is a member of the Alpha Taw Omega Fraternity of the University of Virginia, and the Chicago Athletic Association.

JEROME ROOT,

General Adjuster.

Jerome Root is a native of Schuyler, Herkimer County, New York, and entered the Insurance business in 1857.

J. SHERMAN ROOT,

General Adjuster.

J. Sherman Root was born at De Kalb, Illinois, January 17th, 1867. He was educated in the De Kalb and Chicago public schools and Beloit College at Beloit, Wis. Returning to Chicago, he studied law in the Union College of Law, and was admitted to the bar August 28th, 1889. Subsequently he retired from the law and entered the insurance business with his father in Chicago, May 1st, 1894, under the firm name of Jerome Root & Son.

Mr. Root was married, June 5th, 1895, at Sycamore, Illinois, to Miss Maud B. Ellwood. He is identified with the Masonic order.

CHARLES T. ROTHERMEL,

General Adjuster and Rating Expert.

Charles T. Rothermel was born in Center County, Pennsylvania, December 9th, 1841. Was educated in the public schools and private academies of that state, and graduated in 1859 at the military academy known as "West Branch High School," Jersey Shore, Lycoming County, Pa. Taught school two winters, 1859 and '60 and clerked in his father's general store during the summer. April 18th, 1861, enlisted in Company "A," 34th regiment Pennsylvania Volunteers, and served as a private until June 14th, 1861. July 1st, of the same year, went to Freeport, Illinois, and clerked in a railroad office one year. Entered the Insurance business in 1865 at Freeport, in the office of Winnessheik Insurance Company. Went to Columbus, Ohio, same year and accepted a position as cashier and actuary of the Home Insurance Company, of Columbus, Ohio. Returned to Illinois in 1867 and accepted position of Special Agent of the Ætna Insurance Company, in 1869. Resigned and went with the Western Department of the Putnam Insurance Company, of Hartford, Conn., and remained there until November 1st, 1871; then went to Kansas City, Mo., and engaged in the local business until July, 1874. Returned to Chicago and engaged with the Traders' Insurance Company, and remained there until May, 1882, resigning and accepting position as Compact Manager at Detroit, Michigan, remaining there five years. Returned to Chicago and took up independent adjusting for one year; then accepted position of Secretary of the Buffalo Board of Fire Underwriters, remaining there three years; then went to Louisville, Ky., as Superintendent of Rating in that city, remained one year; then went to Minneapolis and St. Paul in same capacity for one year; then went to Providence, R. I., for one year.

Was married in Wilkesbarre, Pa., February 14th, 1865, to Miss Lizzie B. Nicely. Is a member of the Masonic Fraternity and also the Grand Army of the Republic, U. S. Grant P. st No. 28.

Has rated more cities and towns by schedule than any man in the profession, and is a firm believer in the principles of Schedule Rating, particularly the "Universal Mercantile Schedule."

WILLIAM H. ROTHERMEL,

Special Agent and Adjuster, Traders' Insurance Company of Chicago, Ill.

William Henry Rothermel was born in Jersey Shore, Lycoming County, Penn., April 20th, 1856; removed to Freeport, Ill., with his father, April, 1863. He received his education in the public schools of Freeport, Ill., graduating from the High School in the class of 1876. The same year he engaged in the Lumber business in Freeport, and continued therefor five years, then moved to Chicago and engaged with the Western Department of the Phenix Insurance Company, of Brooklyn, N. Y., where he remained two years. He then returned to the Lumber business at Racine, Wis., remaining three years, then located at Kansas City, Mo., in the same business, remaining there four years, returning to Chicago and conducting a yard at 71st Street and Madison Avenue, disposing of over twenty million feet of lumber in one year for the erection of the World's Fair buildings. In 1893 he engaged with the Traders' Insurance Company in his present position.

September 24th, 1884, he was married to Miss Grace E. Davies, at Racine, Wis., and is the proud possessor of three fine boys.

HUBERT M. RUSSELL,

Special Agent of The New Hampshire Insurance Company.

Hubert M. Russell was born at Russellsburg, Warren County, Pennsylvania, on November 30th, 1839. He first engaged in the dry goods business and entered the insurance business at Galesburg, Illinois, November 1st, 1866, as local agent.

Mr. Russell was married at Galesburg, Illinois, to Miss Sarah M. Sage. He is a member of the Blue Lodge, Chapter Commandery, and Shriner.

L. H. SALOMON,

Insurance Adjuster.

L. H. Salomon was born in Germany on the 9th of October, 1848, and received his education in Germany and France. Mr. Salomon has been engaged in business on three continents, commencing his business career merchandising in Paris, France, following the same business in Algiers, Africa, and entering Insurance at New Orleans, La. He was connected with the Mississippi Valley Insurance Company of Memphis, Tenn., as General Agent for the Western States, and was also in the same capacity for the North German Fire Insurance Company of Hamburg, Germany. From 1887 to 1889 he was with the Lancashire Insurance Company of England, as Assistant to W. G. Ferguson, then General Agent of the Western Department. From 1889 to the present time he has been an Independent Adjuster.

Mr. Salomon was married at New Orleans to Miss Sophie Hamm; they have four children.

(197)

CHARLES FILMORE SIMONSON,

Special Inspector of the Hartford Fire Insurance Company of Hartford, Conn.

Charles Filmore Simonson was born February 16th, 1859, at Brooklyn, N. Y., receiving his education at the public and high schools, and at the Polytechnic Institute of Brooklyn.

He was married, January 14th, 1886, in New York City, to Miss Emma Norah Hornish of Yonkers, N. Y. They have one child, a boy eight years of age.

In October, 1874, Mr. Simonson entered the employ of the Kings County Fire Insurance Company of Brooklyn, and advanced from assistant clerk in the Brooklyn office to chief clerk and bookkeeper in the New York office of this Company. Subsequently he occupied the following positions in the business:

Account Clerk and Daily Report Inspector in the New York office of the Home Insurance Company of New York; then, Special Agent for this Company in Minnesota and Dakota; Special Agent of the Northern Assurance Company of England for Indiana; Eastern Agent at New York of the Western Manufacturers' Mutual Insurance Company of Chicago; afterward appointed Assistant Secretary at Chicago of this Company; General Inspector of the Millers' National Insurance Company of Chicago; Secretary and Manager of the Woodworkers' Mutual Fire Insurance Company of Winona, Minn.; three years ago appointed Expert Underwriter and Inspector of Mill and Factory Hazards for the Hartford Fire Insurance Company at Chicago, which position he now occupies.

Through his connection with the mutual Companies he has been enabled to make a thorough study of mill and factory hazards East and West, which line is now his specialty. He is author of the "Combined Woodworkers', Factory and Warehouse Schedule," which has been approved and adopted for use in the field by several of the leading Companies. He is a member of the Fire Underwriters' Association of the Northwest.

ALONZO D. SMITH,

Examiner of Reports for the Traders' Insurance Company.

Alonzo D. Smith was born in St. Clair County, Illinois, on the 10th of October, 1849, and received his education in the common schools. He entered the Insurance business in 1868 at Springfield, Illinois, as a clerk in a local office, and after various changes incidental to the life of an insurance man now holds the position of Examiner of Reports for the Traders Insurance Company at Chicago. He is personally acquainted with a vast number of Agents East and West.

Mr. Smith is a member of the Iroquois Club and the First Regiment, Illinois National Guard, having been an officer in the regiment twelve years.

THOMAS H. SMITH,

Adjuster of Fire Losses.

Thomas H. Smith was born at Orrington, Penobscot County, Maine, December 12th, 1847. After a high school and academic education he filled various clerkships and was for two years and over with the Merchants Mutual Marine Insurance Company of Bangor; later, for a number of years, in a private bank at Bangor, with which was connected an extensive Local Agency and which turned his attention more particularly to the Fire Insurance business.

In 1873 he came West with the North British and Mercantile Insurance Company as State Agent for Missouri and Kansas; from there he moved to Cincinnati, Ohio, and in 1875, when the Company established a Western Department, he came to Chicago and was connected with the Company in various capacities, first as State Agent and later as Adjuster for the West, until the 1st of January, 1895, when his connection of more than twenty years ceased.

Mr. Smith was married in 1899 to Miss Nellie M. King of Beloit, Wis., and has one child, a boy, now four years old.

He is a member of the Fire Underwriters' Association of the Northwest, and has been for more than twenty years. He is a member of the Union League Club of Chicago, and was for nearly twenty years, prior to the death of Prof. Swing, an attendant upon the Central Church, with which he is still connected.

SYLVANUS HOLBROOK SOUTHWICK,

Adjustor of Fire Losses.

Sylvanus Holbrook Southwick was born at Uxbridge, Mass., January 15th, 1835. He received a Common School education, graduating from Friend's School, Providence, R. I. His early days, after leaving school, were spent at farming, tanning and bricklaying, with his father, and later at shoe manufacturing with his uncle. He is of Quaker descent, his grandfather being a Quaker preacher. He entered the Insurance business at Rockford, Ill., in 1861, and came to Chicago in 1866, since which time he has been constantly engaged in the Insurance business, as Secretary, Local, General and Special Agent and Adjuster.

Mr. Southwick was married at Providence, R. I., December 21st, 1858, to Miss Clara A. Balch, of Providence, R. I., and has one child.

He is a member of the Masonic Landmark Lodge of Chicago.

JOHN R. SUTTON,

Special Agent, Imperial Fire Insurance Company of England.

John R. Sutton was born at Hillsdale, Mich., February 25, 1868. He was graduated from the Ann Arbor University in 1887, and then entered the Insurance business in his native city. Since that time Mr. Sutton has been connected with various Companies in different capacities until he received his present appointment.

In 1890 Mr. Sutton married Miss Gertrude L. March, at Hillsdale, Mich.

A. P. SPENCER,

Adjuster, Queen Insurance Company of America.

A. P. Spencer was born at Eagle Harbor, New York, June 7th, 1846, and was educated at Medina Academy, New York. He entered the Insurance business at Leavenworth, Kansas; was a Local Agent at Peoria, Ill.; Daily Report Examiner of the Hartford Insurance Company; Special Agent of the Imperial and Northern; Special Agent and Adjuster Queen Insurance Company at Kansas City, Mo.; was in Local business at Chicago, being a member of the firm of Spencer & Bissell, Agents for the Western, Home, Hartford, and Anglo-Nevada Insurance Companies; General Western Agent of the City of London Fire Insurance Company at Chicago until its retirement, and is now with the Queen, as Adjuster.

Mr. Spencer was married at Albion, New York, January 11th, 1876, to Miss Marion King, and has four children, three boys and one girl.

CHARLES SQUIRES,

Chief Inspector, Chicago Fire Underwriters' Association.

Charles Squires was born at Marathon, New York, and was educated in the public schools of that place and in a seminary at Painesville, Ohio. He commenced business as a merchandise clerk at Aurora, Illinois, and in 1859 entered the Insurance business at the same place, and in 1860 at Freeport, Illinois. With the exception of a few years in the mercantile business as jobber of saddlery, hardware and leather in Chicago, he has been engaged in the Insurance business most of his business life, first as Solicitor, then as Special Agent, General Agent, State Agent, and Adjuster. Was Secretary of the Continental Insurance Company of Freeport about four years, which he reinsured with the Continental Insurance Company of New York, and he then took their State Agency of Illinois; later on was Adjuster of the Continental for nine States. He has been with the Chicago Underwriters' Association for nearly ten years, first as Manager of the Inspection Department, and at present as Chief of Inspections.

Mr. Squires was married in 1866, at Lockport, New York, to Miss Mary B. Bradshaw, and has one son and one daughter. He is a member of the Kenwood Club and Kenwood Country Club, both of Chicago.

J. H. STEVISON,

Special Agent and Adjuster, Orient Insurance Company of Hartford, Conn.

J. H. Stevison was born in Mount Vernon, Ohio, in 1841. He emigrated to Illinois in 1847 and located at Peoria, being one of the first to enter the first High School established there. He entered the Insurance office of Sweat & Bills, as Clerk in 1858, Peter Sweat retiring in 1860, he became a partner in the firm of Roswell, Bills & Co.

Mr. Stevison enlisted for the War in 1862, serving three years in the field as private, Sergeant, Lieutenant and Captain of Company B, Seventy-seventh Illinois Volunteer Infantry. He was captured at the battle of Mansfield, La., and confined in a rebel prison at Tyler, Texas, for fifteen months, being released at the close of the War, and was then honorably discharged, with the rank of Major for faithful service. Returning to Peoria in 1865, he re-engaged in the Insurance business as partner of Mr. Bills, and so continued until October 1st, 1874, when he disposed of his interest and accepted a position with the Orient Insurance Company of Hartford, as Special Agent and Adjuster in connection with their Western Department at Chicago, where he has remained ever since, over twenty-one years, a long and faithful record, of which he may feel very proud.

WILLIAM H. TAYLOR,

Manager, Loss Department Hartford Fire Insurance Company.

William H. Taylor was born in the village of Argyle, Washington county, N. Y. His education was secured in the village school and academy of his native place. Leaving Argyle he worked in a dry goods store in Troy, N. Y., and later was a salesman in a wholesale dry goods store in New York. In 1857 Mr. Taylor came West and located in Iroquois county, Ill., and when the war broke out was deputy clerk of the circuit court of that county. He enlisted in August, 1862, in the 113th Illinois infantry, third Board of Trade regiment, and served to the close of the war as Regimental Quartermaster. During his residence in Iroquois county, before the war, he was appointed local agent of the Hartford Fire, writing in that company the first policy on the Iroquois court house. After the war he again took up fire insurance and in '67 became an examiner in the Western department of the Hartford. In '76 he succeeded P. C. Royce as state agent for Illinois, which position he retained till the death of C. C. Dana, in the fall of '81, since which time he has been in charge of the loss department. Mr. Taylor has been with the Hartford for almost thirty years and is thoroughly familiar with the business of his department, besides being an all round insurance man. He is a member of he Illinois club, the leading social institution of the West Side and of the Loyal Legion.

RALPH N. TRIMINGHAM,

Secretary of the Chicago Underwriters' Association.

Ralph N. Trimingham was born at St. John's, Newfoundland, September 2d, 1838, and is a member of one of the oldest Colonial families. He was educated at private schools, and at the age of sixteen years he entered upon his business career as clerk in a lawyer's office at St. Vincent, British West Indies. A few years after locating in Chicago he entered the office of Magill & Latham, vessel-owners and commission merchants, with whom he remained for some time. He subsequently became a bookkeeper for his uncle, William Brine, who was a commission merchant, operating upon the Board of Trade. Since 1866 he has been identified with the fire underwriting interests of Chicago. His first connection in that line was with the Home Insurance Company of New York, under the management of Gen. A. C. Ducat, with whom he remained for a little over ten years. After leaving the employ of the Home he was for a short time engaged in mercantile pursuits, but soon re-entered the Fire Insurance business. In 1882 he was elected Secretary of the Underwriters' Exchange, whose members afterwards united with those of the Chicago Board of Underwriters, forming the Chicago Fire Underwriters' Association, he continuing to serve in the same capacity. In 1849 the last named corporation was succeeded by the Chicago Underwriters' Association and Mr. Trimingham was elected Secretary of the new association.

On the 16th of April, 1885, he was married to Miss Carrie J., daughter of Robert G. Goodwillie, an early resident of Chicago. He has been identified with the Masonic order for the last twenty years, being a member of the Cleveland Lodge, Washington Chapter and Siloam Commandery, Knights Templar, of which he is Past Eminent Commander.

EDWIN CHARLES ULRICH,

Independent Adjuster.

Edwin Charles Ulrich was born at Cincinnati, Ohio, on the 2d of August, 1851. He was educated in public and private schools, and commenced his business career in an insurance office at Cincinnati in 1870, and was a Special Agent from January 1st, 1875, to January 1st, 1894, covering eleven states, then becoming an Independent Adjuster in Chicago.

Mr. Ulrich was married at Cincinnati, Ohio, in 1878, to Miss Marie Antoinette Gatti. He is identified with the Knights Templar, Mystic Shrine, and A. O. U. W., National Union.

W. E. VANDEVENTER,

Special Agent and Adjuster, Phoenix Assurance Company of London, Eng.

W. E. Vandeventer was born at Lincoln, Ill., May 18th, 1861, his family removing to St. Louis a few years after. He received his primary education in the St. Louis public schools, graduating from the Washington University. He entered the office of Peugnet & Hemenway, Insurance Agents, in 1880, accepting a minor position, being afterward advanced to chief clerk. He retired from that office to accept a position as General Agency Clerk, in the office of Chas. L. Case, and in 1886 was appointed Special Agent of the Anglo-Nevada for Missouri. In 1887 he accepted a position as State Agent and Adjuster for Missouri, Kansas, Nebraska and Indian Territory, with Col. Wm. Bull, General Agent of several Fire Companies.

In 1890 he was tendered, and accepted, a position as State Agent and Adjuster with the Phoenix Assurance Company, at Chicago, with which company he is now connected. He is an active member of the Central Church, and for several years has been a member of the Executive Committee of the Illinois State Board of Fire Underwriters, is also a member of the Northwestern Association, National Union, Royal League, Legion of Honor, Apollo Commandery Knights Templars, Medinah Shrine, and other secret and beneficiary societies.

FRANK VAN VOORHIS,

General Adjuster.

Frank Van Voorhis was born at Brooklyn, New York, April 19th, 1852. After a few months' service in a leading wholesale cutlery house in New York City he, in January, 1869, began his career in the profession in which he has since continued, with the firm of Skeels, Bowers & Boughton, New York, Local Agents and Brokers, where he remained until April, 1870. In that month he was appointed by the Phenix Insurance Company, of Brooklyn, Assistant Special Agent and Adjuster for the States of Ohio, Indiana and Michigan, with headquarters at Fort Wayne. Advancement quickly followed, and in January, 1874, on the establishment of the Western Department of the Phenix Insurance Company at Chicago, under the management of T. R. Burch, Mr. Van Voorhis was promoted to the position of Special Agent and Adjuster for the State of Michigan, with headquarters at Chicago. Here he remained for three years, and in the fall of '77 was selected to fill the position of General Adjuster for the department. In January, 1881, J. M. Rogers, then Assistant General Agent of the Phenix, resigned that position, and Mr. Van Voorhis was placed in charge of the desk so vacated, which position he retained until January, 1882. He then resigned to accept the managership of the Western Department of the British America Assurance Company, of Toronto, Canada. Ill health compelled him to surrender his charge in July, 1883, and the succeeding eighteen months were spent in part at the seaside, in part at Denver, and among the mountains of Colorado, in an endeavor to recover the strength of which overwork had deprived him.

The fall of 1884 found Mr. Van Voorhis again quartered in Chicago, and in the spring of '85, upon the organization of the Western Adjustment and Inspection Company, he was selected as its manager, resigning December, 1892, and engaging as General Adjuster.

JOHN VIRCHOW,

Special Agent, Prussian National Insurance Company of Germany.

John Virchow is a native of Neufchatel, Switzerland, and was born there July 31st, 1841, when Prussia was in possession of that part of Switzerland. He was educated at the Polytechnical School of Cologne, Prussia, and the University of Bonn, Prussia. After graduating he studied forestry in Germany, and came to America in 1859. Returning to the old country, he entered the Prussian army as a volunteer, serving one year, then came again to this country and served for three years in the United States army, being mustered out in Texas in 1866. For some time after he held the place of clerk in the commissary department at Austin and San Antonio, Texas, then came north to Kansas and entered into the Insurance business with the Kansas Fire and Marine Insurance Company, after resigning from which he was General Agent for the German of Baltimore, then changed to the Hamburg Magdeburg and later to the Fire Insurance Association of England, under Manager Letton, in 1892, and has served under him ever since.

Mr. Virchow was married in San Antonio, Texas, in 1867, to Miss Bertha Weinhold, and has four children.

MILTON PARKER VORE,

Special Agent, The Manchester Fire Assurance Company of England.

Milton Parker Vore was born at Chicago, Illinois, July 21st, 1864, and received his education in the Public, Grammar and High Schools of his native city.

At the age of fifteen, upon the death of his father, he secured a situation in the coffee and spice mills of Thomson & Taylor; six months later he entered the employ of a patent medicine concern, but returned the same year to his former employers, this time being employed in the office. In 1881 he became Assistant Cashier of the Northwestern Masonic Aid Association; then in succession was engaged with the Royal and London and Lancashire, North British and Mercantile, until December 1st, 1890, when he went with the Manchester as Special Agent for Illinois.

Mr. Vore was married at Chicago, September 8th, 1886, to Miss Mary Atwell Ellis; they have three boys.

DAVID S. WAGNER,

Special Agent and Adjuster, Imperial Insurance Company (Limited), of Eng.

David S. Wagner was born in Boone County, Illinois, on the 18th of March, 1848, and is of German descent. His father was drowned at Beloit, Wisconsin, July 9th, 1850, and less than two years later his mother died of typhoid fever, leaving Dave and a sister two years his junior to plough alone; how well he has succeeded must be judged by his many acquaintances. He received his education in the public schools and remained on the farm until seventeen years of age. In May, 1866, he entered the Local Office of the Hartford Insurance Company at Chicago, since which time he has been continuously in the Fire Insurance business, beginning his field work with the Southwick General Agency of the Union of Philadelphia, January 1st, 1875. His first day's service with the Imperial dates December 1st, 1881.

December, 1872, he was married to Miss Virginia C. McIntosh.

SAMUEL W. WARNER,

Special Agent, Mercantile Insurance Company, and American Insurance Company of Boston.

Samuel W. Warner was born in London, England, on the 17th of May, 1859. He commenced his education in the grammar schools of London, and, removing to this country in his boyhood, continued it in the public schools of Chicago. His first business venture was as clerk in a grocery store, afterwards being employed in a civil engineer's office and in the office of John G. Shortall, capitalist, resigning to accept a position as bookkeeper for the Chicago Meat Preserving Company. In August, 1878, he entered the Insurance business with A. T. Smith, General Agent of the Fairfield Fire Insurance Company of Connecticut.

Mr. Warner has been with R. W. Hosmer & Co., General Agents of the Mercantile Fire and Marine Insurance Company and the American Insurance Company of Boston, for a period of fifteen years, and has filled all positions in the profession in both office and field work. At present he attends to the office and field work of both the Companies above mentioned, under management of R. W. Hosmer & Co.

Mr. Warner was married at Chicago in 1882 to Miss Nellie A. Collins, and has five children. He is a member of the Menoken Club and Underwriters' Council of the National Union of Chicago.

HERMANN BUSHROD WASHINGTON,

Adjuster, Hamburg-Bremen Fire Insurance Company of Germany.

Hermann Bushrod Washington was born at Newberry, North Carolina, on the 6th of November, 1848. He was educated by tutors and in private schools. After leaving school he worked four years in a large dry goods house, and at the same time read law under his father. In the year 1870 commenced the Fire Insurance business in the New York office of the Germania Fire Insurance Company, and in 1874 traveled in the Southern States as Special Agent of the New York Underwriters' Agency.

He has been connected with the Chicago office of the Hamburg-Bremen Fire Insurance Company since August 31st, 1892.

Mr. Washington was married to Miss Freida Gerstner of Rastaat, Baden, in the year 1875, and has eight children.

DAVID W. WELLS,

Special Agent and Adjuster for the Fire Association of Philadelphia.

David W. Wells was born in Pittsfield, Berkshire County, Mass., June 28th, 1838, receiving his education in the Grammar and High Schools of his native town. He was employed as bookkeeper for some time, and in 1857 went to Memphis, Tenn., and was there, and in Little Rock, Ark., until the fall of 1860, when he returned to Massachusetts. In June, 1861, he enlisted in the Tenth Massachusetts Regiment, and was in command of a company until disabled from wounds received. He resigned in 1862, and was Secretary and Treasurer of the Santa Fe Stage Company, running a line of stages from Kansas City, Mo., to Santa Fe, Denver, and Old Mexico. From 1867 to 1874 he was in the Watkins Bank, in Kansas City. Then followed one year of Local Insurance business. In November, 1875, he entered the service of the North British and Mercantile Insurance Company, as Special Agent, and after five years' service was appointed Assistant Manager for the same Company at Chicago. In 1884, tired of the confinement of office work, he accepted his present position as State Agent and Adjuster for the Fire Association, of Philadelphia.

Mr. Wells was married at Springfield, Mass., to Miss Frances Crowningshield. They have two daughters. He is a member of the Loyal Legion, Columbia Commandery, Knights Templars, Geo. H. Thomas Post No. 5, G. A. R., Massachusetts Society, Underwriters' Association of the Northwest, and Underwriters' Association of Michigan.

ETHELBERT R. WETMORE,

Special Agent of the New York Underwriters' Agency.

Ethelbert R. Wetmore is a native of Peninsula, Ohio, and was born there February 4th, 1863, receiving his education in the public schools. He entered the Insurance business at Chicago October 23rd, 1883, in the General Agency office of the Germania Fire Insurance Company of New York. During three years with this Company he served on nearly every desk in the office. His health becoming bad, he went to Fargo, North Dakota, and engaged in the drug business for two and a half years; then sold out his interest and returned to Chicago, entering the service of the Orient Insurance Company, one year in the General Agency, receiving appointment as Special Agent for Missouri, Kansas, Indiana and Oklahoma Territory May 12th, 1890; remained in this capacity until March, 1894, when he engaged with the New York Underwriters' Agency as Special Agent, having jurisdiction throughout Chicago and Cook County.

He married Miss Hertha Roesch on the 19th of November, 1890, and has two daughters.

E. S. WHEELER,

Special Agent and Adjuster, The Newark Fire Insurance Company.

Edwin Stewart Wheeler was born at Oregon, Ogle County, Illinois, on the 5th of April, 1858. He was educated in the public schools of Rockford and Chicago, and the Union Law School of Chicago. After graduating he practiced Law for a few years, and in March, 1887, entered the Insurance business with the firm of H. J. Straight & Co., as Special Agent for the People's Fire Insurance Company, of Manchester, N. H., remaining in this position until January 1st, 1889, when he commenced his connection with the Newark.

Mr. Wheeler is a member of the Oddfellows, Knights of Pythias and Masonic Order. He was married September 30th, 1879, at Nora Springs, Iowa, to Miss Chloe I. Gaylord, and had four boys, three of whom are living.

HENRY EUGENE WHITNEY,

Special Agent for the West of the Broadway Insurance Company of New York.

Henry Eugene Whitney was born at Lawrenceville, New York, April 28th, 1856, and was educated in the Chicago and Iowa public schools. He entered the office of F. S. James & Co. at Chicago in 1873 as clerk in the Local Department, remaining there five years and in General Agency office five years. He was then Special Agent under F. S. James for ten years, from 1883 to 1893, Iowa and Nebraska being his territory. On the 1st of March, 1893, he was appointed to his present position, Special Agent for the West of the Broadway Insurance Company of New York.

Mr. Whitney is a Mason, being a member of the Blue Lodge.

EDWIN WASHINGTON WILE,

Superintendent, Cook County Department, Manchester Fire Assurance Company.

Edwin Washington Wile was born at Laporte, Ind., on the 13th of March, 1857, and received his education at Notre Dame University, South Bend, Ind.

In 1876 he entered the General Office of the Phoenix Insurance Company of Hartford at Cincinnati, Ohio. He was afterwards engaged in General Merchandising business at Crookston, Minn., for several years, and then became General Agent for Michigan and Indiana for the Manchester Fire Assurance Company.

His father located in Laporte, Ind., in 1850, where he engaged in the Banking and Insurance business, and conducted one of the oldest and largest Local Agencies in the State.

January 13th, 1884, Mr. Wile was married to Miss Elba Falk of Laporte. He is a member of York Chapter, R. A. M., No. 148; Oriental Consistory Valley of Chicago.

GEORGE A. S. WILSON,

General Adjuster of Fire Losses.

George A. S. Wilson was born at Cincinnati, Ohio, on the 9th of March, 1848, and is of "Quaker" origin. He was educated in the public schools of Cincinnati, and commenced his business life as entry clerk in a wholesale hardware house, and later, was assistant bookkeeper for the largest wholesale and retail dry goods firm of that city, resigning in 1867 to enter the insurance business with J. B. Bennett, General Agent for the Aetna Insurance Company at Cincinnati, remaining with him nine years. He was also connected with the Amazon, Triumph and Andes Insurance Companies as Assistant Secretary, and for ten years acted as Special Agent and Adjuster for leading companies in the Western States, and has occupied every position in the insurance business from Clerk to Secretary, and from Broker to Manager.

Mr. Wilson was married at Cincinnati, Ohio, in 1869, to Miss Alice M. Backman, and has one daughter. He is a member of the Chicago Athletic Club, and the Ohio Society, of Chicago. He has had wide experience as an Adjuster, and has met with success equal to any one in the business. He is well posted in Insurance Law, and is consulted by Lawyers having insurance litigation, in many cases. He has been engaged in every important loss adjustment occurring in Chicago for the past ten years.

JOHN P. WILLIAMS,

Adjuster of Fire Losses.

John P. Williams, the youngest of a family of nine children, was born on the 4th of September, 1832, in Weathersfield, Windsor County, Vt., his father being a farmer. He received a common school education, and when old enough, performed the usual work of a farmer's boy. At the age of seventeen, he taught school winters and worked the farm summers, until 1854, when he took Greeley's advice, and came west, located in Dane County, Wis., and engaged in the mercantile business in 1856; continued in that until 1861, when he enlisted in the Eleventh Wisconsin Infantry for three years. After the Siege of Vicksburg was honorably discharged, returned to Wisconsin and commenced soliciting Insurance for the Northwestern Mutual Life Insurance Company. In 1865 he entered the Local business in Madison, Wis., as senior partner of the firm of Williams & Main, building up one of the largest Agencies in Wisconsin. In 1870 he entered the field As Special agent for the Continental Insurance Company of New York. Continued as Special Agent for several companies until 1883, then went to Omaha, Neb., as State Agent for the Germania Insurance Company of New York, for Nebraska, Kansas, Colorado, Wyoming and New Mexico, remaining there until 1893, then returned to Chicago as c'al Agent for several companies until 1883, then went to Omaha, Neb., as State Agent for Independent Adjuster of Fire Losses. In 1856, he married Miss Mary J. Moseley, of Madison, Wis. They had two daughters. His wife died in 1869, and in 1885 married Miss Margaret A. Durand, of Saginaw, Mich. He has been in the Insurance business continuously for thirty years, either as Local or Special Agent and Adjuster.

I. L. WINN,

Special Agent, Agricultural Insurance Company of Watertown, N. Y.

I. L. Winn was born in Western New York, on the 23d of July, 1837. His parents and grandparents were natives of the vicinity of Newburg, New York, and his great-grandfather was a Revolutionary soldier.

Mr. Winn commenced his business life as a builder, becoming connected with Fire Insurance at Chicago in 1881.

WALTER E. WITHERBEE,

Special Agent. Orient Insurance Company for Wisconsin and Michigan.

Walter E. Witherbee was born on the 19th of May, 1857, at Flint, Michigan, and was educated in the Public Schools. When he was fourteen years old, his father, who was a Banker and Local Insurance Agent at Flint, Mich., died, and the family moved to Caroline County, Maryland, where they lived on a farm for nine years. Mr. Witherbee was first engaged in milling, resigning to enter the book business at Washington, D. C., coming to Chicago in 1882, to pursue the same vocation, becoming eventually a partner in the firm of Brentano & Co., books and stationery, where he remained until 1888 when he resigned to enter the service of the Orient Insurance Company, as Special Agent for Illinois and Indiana. December 22d, 1885, he was married to Miss May F. Paddon.

MORGAN S. WOODWARD,

Associate Manager, Western Adjustment and Inspection Company.

Morgan S. Woodward was born at Davenport, Iowa, March 22d, 1855, and was educated in the Common Schools at Davenport, and at Griswold College. He worked at the trade of machinist at Moline, Illinois, from the time he left school for three and a half years, was then in the United States Naval Service from 1874 to 1879, entered Insurance business in 1880 with the Liverpool and London and Globe Insurance Company, in the Chicago office, as correspondent, then bookkeeper, and later was appointed cashier. Was made State Agent for Iowa and Nebraska in 1886, with headquarters at Des Moines; removed to Chicago again in 1893 as General Adjuster of the Liverpool and London and Globe; resigned December 31st, 1893, to enter the service of the Western Adjustment and Inspection Company, January 1st, 1894.

Mr. Woodward was married at Whitewater, Wisconsin, May 5th, 1880, to Miss Anna G. Graham, and has three children, one son and two daughters. He is a Mason and a member of the Union League Club, Chicago Athletic Association and Royal Arcanum.

(225)

BENJAMIN TAPPAN WRIGHT,
General Adjuster.

Benjamin Tappan Wright was born in Cincinnati, Ohio, on the 6th of December, 1840, and was educated in Cincinnati and Gambier, Ohio. After leaving Gambier he was engaged in the hardware business with the old firms of Tyler, Davidson & Co., and Dickson, Clark & Co., of Cincinnati, and also C. H. Slocomb & Co., of New Orleans. In connection with his accountant work he has handled many lines of goods, among them being hardware, hats, caps and furs, cigars and tobacco and paints and oil. He also taught commercial classes in Bryant & Stratton's Business College, in connection with his accountant examination work. After two years of such work he grew tired of it and gave up teaching. Entering the Insurance field at Chicago in 1873, he has been in it more or less ever since, but only as Adjuster, mainly at first in connection with expert accountant work, but for the last fifteen years almost exclusively as Adjuster.

His grandfather, Judge John C. Wright, was a prominent man in his day in Ohio, and died while President of the Peace Conference, at Washington, D. C., just at the breaking out of the Rebellion. He was one of the proprietors of the Cincinnati Daily Gazette, before it merged into the Commercial Gazette, and was at all times a prominent member of the Ohio bar. Crafts J. Wright, his father, was a graduate of West Point Military Academy in class of '28. He resigned and was associated with his father, in law and newspaper business, until the breaking out of the war, when he was commissioned as Colonel, and afterwards commanded a brigade. After leaving the army he removed to Chicago, where he died.

Benjamin T. Wright was a member of the Old Zouave Guard; he enlisted immediately on the first call, and served in the ranks of the 2d Ohio, and afterwards with the 13th Missouri, and was regularly promoted and resigned as Lieutenant Colonel, commanding the 13th Missouri Volunteers. He then returned to Cincinnati, afterwards went to Kansas and came to Chicago about twenty-four years ago.

Mr. Wright was married at Milwaukee, Wis., in 1863, to Miss Louise Starr, and has two children, both boys. One, John, is an Adjuster in Chicago, and the other, William, is in the Auditing Department of the Wabash R. R. Co., at St. Louis, Mo.

He is Past Master of Garfield Lodge, No. 686, A. F. and A. M.; Past High Priest of Washington Chapter, No. 43, R. A. M.; Chicago Commandery, No. 19, K. T.; also other bodies of the Masonic fraternity. He is also a member of the Society of the Army of the Tennessee, Grant Post, No. 28, G. A. R., and other military societies.

JOHN C. WRIGHT,

Adjuster, Western Adjustment & Inspection Company.

John C. Wright was born at Cincinnati, Ohio, on the 16th of December, 1865, receiving his education in the public schools, finishing with a university course. After leaving the university he entered business as a traveling salesman, eventually connecting himself with the Fire Adjusting business in 1885, at Chicago, with Colonel B. T. Wright, General Adjuster. He was married to Miss Minnie W. Wullweber in 1892 at Chicago, and has one child.

Mr. Wright is connected with several societies in the city of Chicago.

District and County Managers
and Local Agents.

FRANK BARBOUR,

Of the Firm of Granger Smith, Miller & Co., Local Agents.

Frank Barbour was born in Norwalk, Conn., February 28th, 1862. He came West at an early age, and in 1880 began his insurance career in the office of Fisher Bros., from whence he escaped about two years later and engaged with the firm then known as Granger Smith & Miller, of which, for the past seven years he has been a member, under present firm name of Granger Smith, Miller & Co. Mr. Barbour is a member of the Chicago Athletic Association, Kenwood Club, Society of Sons of the American Revolution, and other social organizations.

LOUIS BECKER,

Of the Firm of A. Loeb. Son & Co., Local Agents.

Louis Becker was born in Bavaria, Germany, on the 17th of October, 1853. When he was a child his parents emigrated to America and located in Fort Wayne, Ind., where he received a public school education. He commenced his business life in a Merchant Tailoring and Clothing House, but resigned his position with same to enter the Insurance profession at Goshen, Ind., in 1873.

Mr. Becker was married at Chicago. Ill., January 12th, 1886, to Miss Minnie Loeb. They have one child.

NELSON JAMES BENNETT,

General and Local Agent, Washington Insurance Company of Cincinnati, Ohio.

Nelson J. Bennett was born in Chicago, Ill., on the 20th of August, 1867. He received his education in the public schools of Chicago and after graduating entered the Local Agency office of Hopkins & Hasbrouck on La Salle St., and successively that of A. H. Darrow and the Northern Assurance Company of London. He has been in the business ever since excepting fifteen months, which were spent as clerk in the General Freight Offices of the Chicago & Grand Trunk Ry.

February 5th, 1894, he was married to Miss Katherin E. Lewis of Flint, Michigan, and has one child.

Mr. Bennett is a member of the Royal Arcanum and Royal League.

CHARLES NELSON BISHOP,

Chicago City Manager for the Northern Assurance Company of London, Eng.

Charles Nelson Bishop is a native of Kenosha, Wis., where he was born May 28th, 1855, his father being the Rev. Hiram Nelson Bishop, D. D., rector of St. John's P. E. Church, Chicago. He was educated in the schools of Chicago, and while in the high school edited and published a monthly paper entitled "Little Men." In 1872 he entered the Chicago fire insurance agency of Thomas & W. A. Goodman as clerk, and three years later resigned to enter the service of the "Spectator," in which he was connected in all, though not consecutively, seven years, part of which time as Traveling Agent and part as Manager of its western office at Chicago. From 1880 to 1883, Mr. Bishop lived in Colorado, engaged in mining and publishing the "Summit County Leader," of which he was editor and proprietor. After the following two years at Chicago with the "Spectator," he abandoned journalism to become permanently interested in fire under-writing. He was a partner in the local agency firm of H. H. Brown & Company, of Chicago, from 1885 to 1889, and in the latter year was appointed Chicago City Manager for the Northern of London.

(234)

CHARLES LEWIS BLISS,

Of the Firm of Charles L. Bliss & Co., Local Agents.

Charles L. Bliss was born at Mount Carroll, Carroll County, Illinois, on the 11th of November, 1852; received his primary education in the Public Schools and High School of Freeport, Ill., and was graduated from the Northwestern University, class of '75.

He commenced his business career in the Actuary Department of the National Life Insurance Company of the United States of America, in 1875, at Chicago. January 1st, 1885, he became a partner in the firm of H. J. Straight & Co., and a year later, a partner in the firm of E. W. Lyman & Co. Mr. Rumsey purchased Mr. Lyman's half interest in 1890, and the firm of Rumsey, Bliss & Co. was organized. October 1st, 1892, Mr. Bliss purchased Mr. Rumsey's interest and organized the firm of Chas. L. Bliss & Co., Mr. Bliss being the sole owner of the agency. During all the changes of ownership the companies represented have remained in the agency.

Mr. Bliss was married at Chicago, April, 1878, to Miss Carrie D. Lyon, and has four boys. He is a member of the Grand Lodge of Masons, and Deputy Grand Lecturer for Illinois, also member of the Grand Commandery, Knights Templar, Mystic Shrine, Odd Fellows, Chicago Athletic Club, Oak Park Club and Prairie Club.

WILLIAM F. BRAUN,

Mr. Braun was born at Lawrenceburg, Indiana, November 30th, 1866. After a thorough education in various institutions, he embarked upon a business career as Assistant Cashier of the People's National Bank, which position he resigned in 1890 to accept the Special Agency of the "Old London" for Cook County, in which capacity he has remained ever since.

Upon the removal of the General Agency of the London to New York, in 1892, he was left in charge of all Cook County business, and at this time has supervision of agencies in his district as well as personally attending to all inspections. He is regarded as a pushing yet careful and conservative underwriter.

HENRY HAMILTON BROWN,

Of the Firm of H. H. Brown & Co., Local Agents.

Henry Hamilton Brown was born January 19th, 1832, at Bridgewater, Oneida County, New York. His family came West early in 1839, and located at Peru, Illinois, where he attended the public schools for a while and later entered the Academy at Palatine, Illinois. After leaving the Academy he took up civil engineering; then read law, and in 1856, a good opportunity presenting itself, he entered the insurance business at Peru, representing the Northwestern of Oswego, New York, and the Quaker City of Philadelphia. In July, 1857, he was appointed agent for the Aetna and Hartford Insurance Companies of Hartford, Conn., and in the fall of the same year was appointed Special Agent of the Aetna for Illinois.

In 1862, Mr. Brown moved to Chicago and engaged himself with the firm of L. D. Olmstead & Co., and a year later organized the Garden City Insurance Company, of which company he was secretary until July 1st, 1866, when he resigned and established his present business.

Mr. Brown was married in 1857 to Miss Emily R. Gibbs. He is one of the corporate members of the Illinois Club.

EUGENE POST BURROUGHS,

Of the Firm of A. D. Kennedy & Co., Local Agents.

Eugene Post Burroughs was born at Porterboro, Vermont, on the 7th of February, 1846, receiving his education at the "Troy Conference Academy" of West Poultney, Vermont. He taught school for some time, coming West in 1864, and enlisting in Company A, 138th Illinois Volunteers; was appointed Third Sergeant and soon received the nick-name of "Regulation Sergeant" for strict attention to his duties. After the regiment was discharged, he came to Chicago and entered Bryant & Stratton's Business College, graduating. He then entered the Insurance office of Geo. W. Hayes, at Aurora, Illinois, in 1867, and has been in the Insurance business almost continuously since.

Mr. Burroughs was married at Chicago Oct. 10th, 1869, to Miss Josie E. Miller who died on the 3d of February, 1891. He was married to Miss Perleyette Parmely, his present wife, December 5th, 1893. He has nine children, six girls and three boys, all of whom are living.

Mr. Burroughs is a member of the Menoken Club and attends Grace Baptist Church.

DANIEL W. BURROWS,

General Agent for Cook County for the Insurance Company of North America
and Philadelphia Underwriters.

Daniel Webster Burrows was born at Plymouth, New Hampshire, April 20th, 1855. He was educated for the law, and while studying represented the Home Insurance Company of New York, and several other companies locally. He finally abandoned law to connect himself permanently with Insurance, entering the employ of the Insurance Company of North America as Special Agent in Illinois, and afterward State Agent for territory west of the Mississippi River and following that General Adjuster for the West, and in 1891 was appointed General Agent for Cook County. He has been connected with the Western Department, under J. F. Downing, General Manager of the Insurance Company of North America, for a period of twenty years.

Mr. Burrows is a son of the Hon. Joseph Burrows, one of the leading lawyers and prominent men of New Hampshire. He is a member of the Union, Washington Park, Saddle and Cycle and Chicago Golf Clubs, and the Chicago Athletic Association and Stock Exchange.

PETER FERGUSON CAMERON,

Of the Firm of P. F. Cameron & Co., Local Agents.

Peter Ferguson Cameron was born in Glasgow, Scotland, February 7th, 1859. When he was very young his family came to America and he received his education in the public schools of Hyde Park. In 1870 he entered the office of the Northwestern National Insurance Company, resigning in 1887 to connect himself with the firm of Fred S. James & Co., as Solicitor. In 1890 he established the firm of P. F. Cameron & Co., now sole agents for the Providence-Washington Insurance Company.

April 11th, 1889, he was married at Cincinnati, Ohio, to Mary Adelaide Wynne. They had two children, one of whom is living.

CHARLES HOSMER CASE,

Of the Firm of Case & Co., County Managers, Royal Insurance Company.

Charles Hosmer Case was born in Coventry, Vt., in 1829. His father, a Congregational clergyman, was one of the pioneers in Northern Vermont. His family being large, and the salary of the good pastor small, the children were thrown upon their own resources at an early age.

Mr. Case was educated in the Public Schools and also under private tutelage at home. At fifteen we find him a clerk in a store in his native town, where he began at the princely salary of $75 a year, which figure, however, was raised several times. During his four years' stay in the store, by dint of strict economy he saved enough to pay for a four years' course in the academical institution at Bakersfield, Vt.

In 1852 Mr. Case bade adieu to the Green Mountains and set out for the West, locating at Warsaw, Illinois, where he presided over a private academy for two years. Next he engaged in the hardware business at that place, at the same time conducting a local fire insurance agency. In '61 he was appointed Illinois Special Agent for the Home of New York, remaining with it four years, during which time he was stationed for a season at the then St. Louis General Agency. Upon resigning his position with the Home he identified himself with the Insurance Company of North America as Assistant General Agent and Adjuster. In 1871 he became Western Manager of the Royal Insurance Company, and several years later was appointed General Agent for the London and Lancashire as well. He was also Local Agent for these and other companies. He was President of the "Union" and has held various offices of trust outside of insurance. He was President of the Chicago Newsboys' Home for three years, and has been President of the Washingtonian Home for twenty years, and has represented his ward in the City Council from '75 to '77. He is also a member of the Union League Club and the Citizens' Association.

In religious work, also, he is prominent, being Superintendent of the Sunday School and a member of the Prudential Committee of the First Congregational Church, and a corporate member of the American Board of Foreign Missions.

(241)

EDWARD B. CASE,

Of the Firm of Case & Co., County Managers of the Royal Insurance Company.

Edward B. Case was born at Boston, Mass., February 2d, 1853, and attended the Public Schools of Cambridge and Phillips' Academy of Andover, Mass. In 1868 he entered the Insurance office of Case & Heywood, as office boy, remaining there one year, then resigned to return East and complete his education. He entered Yale College in 1873, but finally abandoned a university career, and again connected himself with Insurance at Chicago, in the office of his uncle, C. H. Case, and has been with him ever since, occupying every position in the office from office boy to his present position. He is a brother of Chas. L. Case, United States Manager of the London Assurance, and Frank C. Case, an Insurance Agent at St. Louis, Mo.

Mr. Case married Miss Lilly Prentiss, daughter of the Rev. N. A. Prentiss, of Aurora, Ill., in 1880, and has four children. He resides at Evanston, Ill., and is a member of the Evanston and Country Clubs, as well as the Society of Colonial Wars and the Union League Club of Chicago.

JOSEPH H. CHAMBERLIN,

Insurance Agent.

Joseph H. Chamberlin was born in Schenectady, New York, but came at an early age with his father's family to Illinois. His youth was spent on a farm near Sterling, White-side County, Illinois.

After one year's attendance at the Lutheran College at Mendota, he began a course of teaching and studying until in the year of 1882, when he graduated from the Law Department of the University of Michigan at Ann Arbor.

Returning to Sterling he went into partnership with his brother, who was conducting a real estate and insurance business at Sterling. Taking charge of the insurance branch of the business, he was elected secretary of the local board of underwriters. In a short time he built up an agency having the largest business in the county, the firm being sole agents for twenty of the leading foreign and American companies.

After five years' experience in the business at Sterling, he disposed of his interest in the firm and removed to Chicago. In the year 1889 he entered into partnership with Wm. C. Magill, under the style of Magill & Chamberlin, continuing business in this way until November 1st, 1895, since which time he has been carrying on business in his own name.

JOSEPH J. COFFEY.

Of the Firm of Loeb & Coffey, Local Agents.

Joseph J. Coffey was born in Chicago, Illinois, May 1st, 1871, receiving his education in the schools of his native city. He has always been an insurance man, entering the business in 1888, in the office of Thos. and W. A. Goodman, and remaining there continuously until the formation of the firm of Loeb & Coffey. He is a member of the Columbus Club of Chicago.

EUGENE COWAN,

Of the Firm of Cowan & Van Every, Local Agents.

Eugene Cowan was born at Greenwich, New York State, January 8th, 1842, of Scotch descent. He attended the public schools and completed his education at Greenwich Academy. He left school and enlisted in the One Hundred and Twenty-third New York Infantry Volunteers, August 7th, 1862; served through the war and was discharged near Washington, D. C., June 8th, 1865. He then entered the Insurance business in the office of W. J. Whaling & Co., at Milwaukee, Wis.

Mr. Cowan was married at Geneva, Illinois, December 25th, 1869, to Miss A. L. Belden, and has two children living. He is a member of the Menoken Club and Geo. H. Thomas Post, No. 5, G. A. R.

JOHN CRITCHELL,

Of the Firm of R. S. Critchell & Co., Local Agents.

John Critchell was born at Rochester, New York, October 17th, 1847, and was educated in the Public Schools of Cincinnati.

He entered the Insurance business in 1860, in the General Office of the Aetna Insurance Company, at Cincinnati, Ohio. In 1872 he was married to Miss Rebecca G. Henry, at Carthage, Ohio. He is a member of the Chicago Athletic Club, and is a York and Scottish Rite Mason.

ROBERT MOODEY CRITCHELL,

Of the Firm of R. S. Critchell & Co., Local Agents.

Robert Moodey Critchell was born at Chicago, Illinois, on the 12th of October, 1871. He was educated in the Chicago Public Schools and High Schools and Chicago Manual Training School. After completion of college preparation, and having the option of a college or business career, he chose business, and entered the employ of the Insurance Company of the State of Pennsylvania, as bookkeeper in 1889.

In 1893 he became a member of the firm of Geo. C. Clarke & Co., and a year later became a partner in the firm of R. S. Critchell & Co.

Mr. Critchell was married at Chicago to Miss Mary Powell, and has one child. He is a member of the Chicago Athletic Association and the Kenwood Country Club.

THOMAS SCOTT CUNNINGHAM,
Of the Firm of Thomas S. Cunningham & Co.

Thomas Scott Cunningham was born on March 25th, 1835, at Harrisburg, Penn. He was educated in the Public Schools of his native town, and had his first business training in the locomotive works of Richard Norris & Son, at Philadelphia, where he received a thorough course in practical and theoretical mechanics, and was engaged in the designing and construction of locomotives from 1851 to 1859, at which time he withdrew, to enter the naval service of the United States, as third assistant engineer. Admission was by examination, and the fact that he emerged from the ordeal at the head of the class of twenty-six young men, serves to illustrate how devoted and earnest he had been in the study of his profession. His first assignment was to the steam sloop of war Lancaster, which was made the flag-ship of the Pacific Squadron, until 1861, when, having been advanced to the grade of second assistant engineer, he was ordered home to participate in the crushing of the Rebellion, and was detailed in charge of the engineering department of the gunboat Wissahickon. In that famous warship Mr. Cunningham served one year as senior engineer in the squadron of Admiral David G. Farragut. Returning North in September, 1862, to repair damages sustained by vessel and machinery in that arduous campaign, he was detailed by the Secretary of the Navy to the staff of Rear Admiral Francis H. Gregory, then in supervision of the bureau of construction of monitors, ironclads, gunboats and their machinery, at New York. The work of this bureau ceasing with the close of the Rebellion, Mr. Cunningham resigned from the service in November, 1866, and returned to civil life, holding President Johnson's commission as a first assistant engineer, with the rank of Lieutenant, to which grade he was advanced in July, 1866. He afterward took the general management of the New York branch of the Hartford Steam Boiler Inspection and Insurance Company, and was so identified until the spring of 1873. On March 12th of that year, he came to Chicago as a member of the insurance firm of W. H. Cunningham & Co., the senior member of which was his brother. Their business connection continued until October, 1884, when Mr. Cunningham withdrew, and established himself alone. He is a thorough business man, of ample experience in his profession, and an expert underwriter. He is a member of the Military Order of the Loyal Legion, the Union League Club, the Farragut Veteran Association and Apollo Commandery, No. 1, K. T. Mr. Cunningham was twice married, and has two children—a son and a daughter.

SECOR CUNNINGHAM,

Local Agent.

Secor Cunningham was born at Altoona, Pennsylvania, May 24th, 1864, and was educated in different private academies. He entered the Insurance business with his father, Thomas S. Cunningham, at Chicago, on the 1st of October, 1880.

Mr. Cunningham is a member of the Chicago Athletic Club.

HERBERT DARLINGTON,

Of the Firm of Darlington, Harvey & Co., Local Agents.

Herbert Darlington was born at West Chester, Penn., February 25th, 1851. His family are all good Quakers, who came over here about 1700, and settled near Philadelphia. After attending a private school he entered the preparatory department of Griswold College, Davenport, Iowa, leaving to go to work, at the age of fifteen, when half through his collegiate course. He engaged in business with the insurance firm of I. F. Dobson & Co., in the Chamber of Commerce Building at Chicago, on the 6th of November, 1866.

Mr. Darlington was married on the 15th of February, 1876, and has five children. He is in his fourth term as treasurer of the Iroquois Club and is a member of the LaGrange Club.

HARRY C. DANA,

Of the Firm of Williams, Dana & Deems, Local Agents.

Harry C. Dana was born at Rochelle, Illinois, on the 4th of August, 1861, receiving his education in the grammar and private schools at Chicago. After completing his education he traveled for the firm of M. D. Wells & Co., wholesale boots and shoes, and has been in the insurance business about eight years; first with the Aetna Insurance Company, and then with Moore & Janes, later becoming a member of the firm of Williams, Dana & Deems. He was married February 17th, 1892, at Chicago, to Miss Margaret Williams, and has one child—a son.

Mr. Dana lives at Hinsdale, Illinois, and is a member of the Hinsdale Club.

LEWIS H. DAVIS.

Lewis H. Davis was born August 19th, 1833. His parents were Clark and Ellie Fancher Davis, his father of English descent and his mother of French. For three generations, however, his family have been Americans, and our subject has always been intensely American. From his youth he was uninterruptedly kept in school, under patient and competent teachers. He entered the academy at Amsterdam, N. Y., in 1849, and continued there until 1851, when he entered last term freshman in Madison University, now Colgate University. He graduated in August, 1854, just before he was twenty-one, and immediately entered upon the study of law in Utica, N. Y., and in 1855 was admitted to the bar, while studying with Roscoe Conkling. In August, 1856, he came to Chicago and entered upon the practice of law in the office of Hon. N. B. Judd, and in March, 1858, was elected to the office of Magistrate, running largely ahead of his ticket. During the first year of his incumbency he disposed of over thirty-three hundred cases and presided with so much dignity and evinced so much learning in the law that he was at once crowned Judge by the Chicago bar. During his term of office he was a candidate for judge, and failed of the nomination by a small majority, the successful nominee being afterwards elected by an overwhelming vote. He subsequently filled the offices of United States Pension Agent and Fire Commissioner, and while filling the latter office it was largely due to Lewis H. Davis that the city of Chicago now has the best water supply and the best Fire Department, equipped with the best fire engines and the best hose of any city in the world. While practicing law he was associated with some of the ablest lawyers of the Chicago bar. The law firms were: Buell & Davis; Peck, Buell & Davis; Davis & Adams; Adams & Davis (now Judge Adams), and Davis & Schuyler, now of the firm of Schuyler & Kramer.

July 1st, 1866, our subject purchased a half interest in the established fire insurance agency of Alfred James, and formed a partnership of James & Davis. The General Agency of the Liverpool and London and Globe was urged upon the firm, but was respectfully and reluctantly declined. Subsequently Mr. James removed to New York and the firm of Davis, James & Co., composed of Lewis H. Davis, Fred S. James and S. F. ReQua, was established. On the 1st day of July, 1871, the firm of Davis & ReQua was established and continues to-day, the oldest unchanged agency in Chicago. The firm of Davis & ReQua have paid the companies represented by them since the October fire of 1871, the handsome sum of over $1,300,000 net, over and above all losses and expenses. Mr. Davis was married in July, 1860, to Miss Harriet W. Farlin, daughter of Mrs. M. B. Farlin, widow of Myron B. Farlin, of Quebec, who had large interest in the lumber business. He built him a residence at No. 1458 Michigan Avenue, in 1866, where he and his wife still live. No children ever blessed their union.

Mr. Davis has always taken a prominent and leading part in all the Underwriters' Boards and Associations since 1866. He went to Springfield in the session of the Legislature in 1869, and was successful in placing upon the statute books what is termed the Insurance laws of 1869. Mr. Davis is a member of the Second Presbyterian Church, the Union League and Chicago Clubs. He has acquired a competence; is a liberal giver, contributing yearly to over thirty different benevolent institutions. He is a man in his full physical and mental vigor, and has every promise of active business life for many years to come.

LEWIS H. DAVIS,

Of the Firm of Davis & ReQua. Local Agents.

HARVEY DEAN,

Of the Firm of Moore & Janes, Local Agents.

Harvey Dean was born at Xenia, Ohio, on the 27th of November, 1851, and was educated in the Chicago public schools. He entered the Insurance business in the office of S. M. Moore & Co., on the 1st of September, 1872, at Chicago, Ills., and is now with the firm of Moore & Janes, of the same place.

Mr. Dean is a member of the Royal Arcanum, National Union, and Congregational Club. He was married at Council Bluffs, Iowa, January 5th, 1882, to Miss Julia M. Guernsey, and has four children.

HARRY WILLIAM DEEMS,

Of the Firm of Williams, Dana & Deems, Local Agents.

Harry William Deems was born at St. Louis, Missouri, on the 24th of August, 1861, receiving his education in the Public Schools of that city. For some years he was connected with the Wood and Willowware business, but becoming interested in Insurance he retired from that, and entered the Western Department of the Lancashire Insurance Company, in January, 1882, remaining with said Company until January 1st, 1891. He was then chief of the Oakland Home Insurance Company—1891 and 1892—and Assistant Manager of the same company until they re-insured on the 1st of January, 1894. Mr. Deems then formed a partnership with H. N. Williams (the former manager of the Oakland Home Insurance Company) for the local business, under the firm name of Williams & Deems.

Mr. Deems is identified with several Masonic organizations in Chicago, a member of the National Union and the Fire Underwriters' Association of the Northwest. He was married at Carlinville, Illinois, to Miss Minnie Bates, and has three children.

(255)

HOLGER DE ROODE,
Western Fire Underwriter.

Holger de Roode was born at Rotterdam, Holland, October 22d, 1853. He came to this country at an early age and received his education principally at St. Xavier's College, of Cincinnati, O. Mr. De Roode entered a fire insurance office when less than sixteen years of age, and has been continuously in business twenty-six years, and in the local business in Chicago twenty-two years. Meanwhile he was General Manager at Chicago of the Clinton Fire of New York, the Southern California, and Providence-Washington Insurance Companies. He was the pioneer in the co-insurance movement and chairman of the first committee of the Western Union on that subject. Mr. De Roode is Vice-President of the Chicago Society for Ethical Culture, and has been a frequent contributor to the Insurance Press and the proceedings of the Fire Underwriters' Association of the Northwest. He is now conducting a General Insurance Agency in Chicago, in fire, life and other branches, representing principally the Liverpool & London & Globe, and the New England Mutual Life of Boston, in addition to the care and management of certain estates.

March 26th, 1879, he was married at Chicago to Miss Cornelia M. Volwider, and has four children. He is a member of the Union League Club of Chicago, St. George's Club of London, England, and various insurance organizations.

(256)

CHARLES WILSON DREW,

Of the Firm of Charles W. Drew & Co.

Charles Wilson Drew was born in Meridian, Cayuga County, New York, on the 19th of April, 1835. He lived on a farm until he was fifteen years of age, receiving his education in the Common Schools and Academy. He commenced his business career as clerk in the book store of John Ivison, at Auburn, New York. In 1854, he went overland to California, returning home, via the Isthmus in 1859. After two years in business, he joined the army in 1861, where he remained until the close of the war, when he removed to Chicago and entered the Insurance business.

Mr. Drew married Miss Anna S. Fleetwood in 1867; they have one daughter. He is a member of the Calumet, Washington Park and Union League Clubs.

ARTHUR CHARLES DUCAT,

Of the Firm of Ducat & Lyon, Local Agents.

Gen. Arthur Charles Ducat was born in Dublin, Ireland, on the 24th of February, 1830. His father, Mungo Moray Ducat, was a gentleman who traced his lineage from a very ancient Highland family, renowned in the annals of Scotland. Arthur C. Ducat was educated at private schools in his native city, and at the age of nineteen came to America with the intention of becoming a civil engineer. He pursued that profession for some years on important railway lines and other public works. This occupation was abandoned when he was tendered the position of Secretary and General Surveyor of the Board of Underwriters of Chicago, which position he accepted and occupied until the opening of the Civil War. In the meantime he began to manifest a keen interest in the city affairs, and organized, drilled and disciplined the Citizen's Fire Brigade, a semi-military and armed body of citizens. At the breaking out of the war he enlisted as a private in the Twelfth Illinois Infantry in April, 1861, going all through the war, with promotion at intervals until he arrived at the rank of General.

Soon after the close of hostilities, the Home Insurance Company of New York appointed him to superintend its business in Ohio, Indiana and Kentucky, and shortly afterwards he became its General Agent in Chicago. His career as an active Underwriter has been eminently successful. The firm of Ducat & Lyon, of which he is the head, carries on a general fire insurance business. One of the standard works of America is "Ducat's Practice of Fire Underwriting," which he brought out in 1875. In 1886 he was elected commander of the Illinois Commandery of the military order of the Loyal Legion. He is a member of the Grand Army of the Republic, and of the Masonic Order, being identified with the Apollo Commandery, Knights Templars, and is a member of the Chicago Club. He was married to Miss Mary Lyon, daughter of William Lyon, Esq., of Bedford., Penn. Her death occurred at Chicago October 26th, 1890, and in 1892 he was married to Miss Alice Jane Soutar, daughter of P. J. Soutar, an eminent lawyer of Dunfermline, Scotland.

WILLIAM H. EBBERT,

Of the Firm of Munger, Ebbert & Co.

William H. Ebbert was born at Chicago on the 10th of June, 1854, and was educated in the Public Schools of his native City.

In May, 1871, he entered the insurance business in the office of the Globe Insurance Company of Chicago. In 1877 he entered the employ of D. S. Munger, and in 1887 was given an interest with D. S. Munger, under the firm name of D. S. Munger & Company, and in January, 1893, the firm name was changed to Munger, Ebbert & Co.

He was married on the 19th of June, 1879, to Miss Nellie J. Swenie, daughter of Chief Swenie of Chicago, and has nine children. He is a member of the Royal Arcanum, Royal League, National Union, Sheridan Club and Columbus Club.

Mr. Ebbert's father is eighty-two years old, hale and hardy. He comes down to his son's office daily, walking from his home on Ashland avenue

ALFRED R. EDWARDS,

Of the Firm of Edwards, Morse & Kloo. Local Agents.

Alfred R. Edwards is a native of Berlin, Connecticut. He was educated in the Public Schools, and entered the Fire Insurance business on Wall Street, New York City, remaining in it continuously ever since. He was married at Meriden, Connecticut.

GEORGE ESSIG,

Of the Firm of George M. Harvey & Co.

George Essig was born at Memphis, Tenn., on the 16th of October, 1860. After completing his education, which he received in the public schools of Memphis, he embarked on a mercantile career, later taking up merchandise brokerage. Some years later he became interested in Insurance, and resigning the position which he then held, in 1884 he entered the profession with the firm of George M. Harvey & Co., at Chicago.

Mr. Essig is a member of the Chicago Athletic Association.

ROBERT WESLEY FAULKNER,

Of the Firm of Straight & Lyman. District Managers.

Robert Wesley Faulkner was born in Milwaukee, Wis., in the year 1852, and received his education in the Public and High Schools of that city. He came to Chicago in 1875 and for some years held a responsible position with a large Board of Trade firm. In 1876 he connected himself with the Insurance firm of Straight & Lyman as general bookkeeper and cashier and after two years of faithful service resigned to accept a similar position with another Board of Trade firm.

In 1884 he returned to the firm of Straight & Lyman, where he still remains, being in charge of the County Department and general outside work. Mr. Faulkner is a married man and the proud father of three promising boys.

FRANCIS PORTER FISHER,

Of the Firm of Fisher Bros., Local Agents.

Francis Porter Fisher was born at Oswego, New York, May 19th, 1828. He comes of New England stock, his ancestors coming over between 1630 and 1640. He spent three years in France with his father's family, from 1839 to 1842, attending school most of the time, being fitted for college at Williston Seminary, Easthampton, Mass., and graduating at Harvard University in 1848. After reading law for awhile, he entered the office of the Northwestern Insurance Company of Oswego, New York, in January, 1851. In 1854 he engaged in the business of getting out square timber in Northern Michigan, and shipping to the Chicago market, in connection with his brother, but closed the business in 1857. In 1859 he joined a United States exploring party to New Mexico and Utah, known as the United States San Juan Expedition. In 1860, was engaged as Civil Engineer in connection with the Texas and New Orleans Railroad, in Eastern Texas. Enlisted as a private in Company C, Fifty-fifth Illinois Volunteer Infantry, at Chicago, November 1st, 1861, was promoted to Commissary Sergeant, and in 1863 to First Lieutenant and Adjutant of the Fifty-fifth Illinois Volunteer Infantry, and participated in all movements of the regiment from Shiloh to Atlanta, and was mustered out at Chattanooga, Tenn., October 31st, 1864, by reason of expiration of term of service, three years. Then he entered the employ of the Lumbermans' Insurance Company of Chicago in September, 1865, and after the fire of 1871, became Local Agent of the Farragut of New York, which company he has represented for twenty-three years. In 1875, he formed a partnership with his brother Frederic, in the Fire Insurance business, under the firm name of Fisher Bros., which partnership was terminated by the death of his brother, March 28th, 1886, since then the business has been continued under the same style.

Mr. Fisher was married at Oswego, N. Y., January 26th, 1853, to Miss Ann Eliza Crane. He is a member of the Athletic Club, Harvard Club, Loyal Legion (Illinois Commandery), Thomas Post, No. 5, G. A. R., Sons of the American Revolution, Society of Colonial Wars, Society of the Army of Tennessee, Society of Fifty-fifth Illinois Volunteer Infantry, and Salon Francais.

STANLEY FLEETWOOD,

Of the Firm of Charles W. Drew & Co.

Stanley Fleetwood was born in New York City in the year 1847, but moved to Chicago in 1856, and has resided here continuously ever since, receiving his education in the private schools, Douglas University and Racine College, Wisconsin. In 1868 he entered the employ of the Illinois Central Railroad Company in their general office in Chicago, resigning to accept a position in the wholesale dry goods house of Bowen, Whitman & Winslow, afterward being connected with the wholesale dry goods house of Marshall Field & Co., which, in 1883, he left to become a member of the firm of Chas. W. Drew & Co.

He was married in January, 1883, to Miss January, of Kentucky, and has one child.

PATRICK H. FLEMING,

Of the Firm of P. H. Fleming & Co.

Patrick H. Fleming was born at Chicago, Illinois, on the 15th of March, 1860, receiving his education in the grammar schools and taking a business course in Bryant & Stratton's Business College.

In 1872 he entered the office of Farmer, Atkins & Co., as office boy, rising from that position to clerk, partner and successor. Mr. Fleming has represented as General Western Agent the Lehigh Valley Transfer Company, is now General Agent of the Union Marine Insurance Company of Liverpool, England, for ocean and lake marine, and is also a Vessel Agent, Freight Broker and Vessel Owner. He has been in the Insurance business on La Salle Street for over twenty years and is well known to all old timers.

Mr. Fleming is a member of the Athletic, Germania and Ashland Clubs, and also of the Board of Fire Underwriters, Board of Marine Underwriters, Chicago Stock Exchange and Board of Trade.

STUART WHITNEY FRENCH,

Of the Firm of Steward, French & Co., Local Agents.

Stuart Whitney French was born at Dansville, Livingston County, New York, on the 12th of February, 1867. When he was a boy his family removed to Chicago and he received his primary education in the Chicago Public Schools, and graduated from Amherst College, Amherst, Mass., class of '89. He commenced his business life in the local office of Ducat, Lyon & Co., remaining with this firm eighteen months, then becoming Special Agent of the London Assurance Company. After two years' special experience he went with the North British, as assistant to Resident Secretary Glidden, engaging with his present firm, August 1st, 1894.

Mr. French is a grandson of Sireno French, son of B. W. French, General Agent, and brother of Chas. B. French, Assistant Manager of the Manchester Insurance Company. He was married December 27th, 1894, to Miss Helen S. Stevison. He is a member of the Alpha Delta Phi Fraternity, and is Secretary of the Western Alumni Association of Amherst College.

THOMAS ELWOOD FRY,

Of the Firm of Hammond, Fry & Sheldon.

Thomas Elwood Fry was born at Bolton, Worcester County, Mass., on the 17th of June, 1834, and is of Quaker origin. He was educated in the Common Schools and High School of Bolton, commencing business in a beef and pork packing house. He went to Kansas at the time of "Border Ruffian" troubles, and voted against the notorious "Lecompton Constitution," about an hour after arriving in the state, "Jim Lane" telling him he was a good enough citizen by that time. He later returned East and resided in Brooklyn and New York, coming to Chicago in 1865, and entering the Insurance business with Davis, James & Co., in 1868. In 1881 he formed a partnership with L. D. Hammond, now the firm of Hammond, Fry & Sheldon.

Mr. Fry was married to Miss Clara W. Thurston, at Lynn, Mass., on the 30th of October, 1862, and has one son grown up and married.

Mr Fry is a member of Unity church (Unitarian), and belongs to the Massachusetts Society and the Chicago Whist Club.

(267)

M. L. C. FUNKHOUSER,

Of the Firm of George W. Montgomery & Co.

M. L. C. Funkhouser was born at St. Louis, Mo., January 17th, 1864. His father, Robert M. Funkhouser, was for years conspicuous in St. Louis business circles. He conducted one of the largest dry goods houses on the Mississippi River, and was once President of the Chamber of Commerce, and interested as a director or stockholder in various institutions. Mr. Funkhouser was seventeen years old when he left the high school to enter the local Fire Insurance offices of W. G. Bentley & Co., in St. Louis, where he remained three months as an office boy. After that he became a collector for the Singer Manufacturing Company; then tried his luck in New Orleans for a while; and then returning to St. Louis, engaged for a few weeks in the express business. In September, 1884, he came to Chicago, and worked for two months with the firm of C. H. Koch & Co., and on the 1st of the following December entered the office of George W. Montgomery & Co., which firm became General Agents for the West of the Fidelity & Casualty, in September, '86, Mr. Funkhouser being made Assistant Western General Agent on January 1st, '88. He continued as such until July 1st, 1889, when he was made one of the General Agents and admitted to partnership in both the Local Fire and General Agency business.

JAMES S. GADSDEN,

General Agent of the Aetna Insurance Company.

James S. Gadsden was born at Northall, England, on the 28th of January, 1835, receiving his education in private schools in England. After leaving school he was employed upon his father's farm for a time, and later studied law in the offices of John Becke and Wilson Bros., being admitted to practice in 1857, and continuing until 1864. He then connected himself with the Aetna Insurance Company of Hartford, Conn., removing to and entering the Cincinnati branch of said company, of which J. B. Bennett was then General Agent. He was Superintendent of the Sub-Agency (called General Agency) Department until ill-health caused him to seek change of duties, and after adjusting an occasional loss, he went, in the latter part of December, 1865, to assist F. C. Bennett in the adjustment of the Company's losses in the large conflagration at Vicksburg, Miss., and in January, 1866, at Grenada, Miss. In 1866 or 1867, he succeeded to the Illinois State Agency of the Aetna. In 1871 he removed to Chicago as General Adjuster for the Aetna, and later assisted in the adjustment of the Company's losses by the great fire of October 8th and 9th, 1871, involving 1,808 policies, and a net loss payment of $3,783,000.

He continued as General Adjuster until October, 1885, when he succeeded to the General Agency of the Chicago branch of said Company, to which was added, in the spring of 1891, the General Agency of the Lake Marine Department, covering Lakes Michigan, Huron, Erie, Ontario and Superior, and their tributaries, and which position he now occupies.

Mr. Gadsden is a member of the Apollo Commandery, Knights Templar, and of the Illinois Club. He was married in Delaware County, Iowa, July 4th, 1856, to Miss F. S. McKee.

ORLANDO CHARLES GAY,

City Manager, Phenix Insurance Company of Brooklyn, N. Y.

Mr. Gay was born in Carmel, Putnam County, New York, February 24th, 1850, of American parents. In the early '50's his parents came West and settled in Columbus, Wisconsin, afterwards removing to Racine, where he attended the High School. At the age of fourteen he removed to Delavan, same State, completing his education at that place in the line of civil engineering, and graduating with high honors in his class.

After graduating he accepted a position on the engineering corps of the New York State Canal. This life was not compatible with the ambition of young Gay, and the field was not large enough for him, and in looking around in order to better himself, his choice fell upon Fire Insurance, as better suited to his taste. That the choice was a judicious one, his career since he entered the business proves beyond a doubt. In 1869 he accepted a position with the Mutual Security Insurance Company, at Chicago, Illinois. At the time of the great fire in 1871, he was connected with the Insurance Agency of H. S. Tiffany & Co. After four years' connection with that firm was employed in the Traders' office of Chicago, and in March, 1886, entered the employ of the Phenix Insurance Company of Brooklyn, New York, where by strict attention to business he shortly assumed the management of the City Department.

February 16th, 1887, he married Miss Laura Virginia Claybourne, at Milwaukee, Wisconsin. Socially, Mr. Gay is a hale-fellow-well-met, and the Oakland Club and the Royal Arcanum Home Council have the privilege of numbering him among their members.

(270)

THOMAS GOODMAN,

Of the Firm of Thomas & W. A. Goodman, Local Agents.

Thomas Goodman was born at Market Harborough, England, February 2, 1816, and emigrated in 1832, leaving London on July 26, in the good ship Columbia. He reached New York on September 7, which in those days was considered a splendid voyage. He settled in Canton, Ohio, and after leaving school he was for a time employed in a bank and later as clerk of the Supreme Court. He then studied law and was admitted to the bar in July, 1845. The same year he accepted the Secretaryship of the Stark County Mutual Insurance Company, which after four years' of service he resigned and was appointed Special Agent of the Hartford Fire for Northern Ohio. He came to Chicago for this Company in 1861 and two years later resigned and organized the Lumberman's of Chicago, of which he was first the Secretary and later on the President until 1870, when he withdrew and established a local agency.

Mr. Goodman was married in Canton, Ohio, in 1838, to Miss Hannah Jane Saxton, the only daughter of John Saxton, the pioneer editor of the Ohio Repository. He has eight children and fifteen grandchildren all alive and well. He has always been a stanch member of the church, first in Canton, Ohio, and later in Chicago, and is also the President of the Old Tippecanoe Club of Chicago.

LYMAN DRESSER HAMMOND,

Of the Firm of Hammond, Fry & Sheldon, Local Agents.

Lyman Dresser Hammond was born on the 31st of October, 1844, at Amherst, Mass., being a descendant of Thomas Hammond, who came from Lavenham, England, and settled in Hingham, Mass., in 1636; of Richard Lyman, one of the original proprietors of Hartford, Conn., and who died there in 1641, and of John Dresser, who died at Rowley, Mass., in 1672. Many of the descendants of these colonists took active part in establishing the independence of this country.

Mr. Hammond was educated in the Common Schools of his native town and at Hopkin's Academy of Hadley, Mass. After leaving school he was on a farm at Hadley for some time, and when about twenty years of age, ran a steam ferry on the Connecticut River, at Hockanum, Mass. During the winters of 1865 and 1866 he taught school, giving this up to come West. He settled in Warsaw, Illinois, and for three years was engaged in the grain and milling business at that place. In the fall of 1869 he came to Chicago and commenced his long connection with the insurance business in the office of C. H. Case, where he remained six years. At the end of that time he was appointed agent of the British America Assurance Company of Toronto, Canada, which Company he has represented continuously up to the present time, a period of over twenty years. On the 21st of November, 1871, Mr. Hammond was married to Miss Harriet Elizabeth Barstow and has two children. He is a member of the Union League Club, Illinois Club, Kenwood Club, Society of Colonial Wars, Sons of the American Revolution, and Sons of Massachusetts.

CYRUS AUSTIN HARDY,

Of the Firm of Edward M. Teall & Co., Local Agents.

Cyrus A. Hardy was born on the 7th of February, 1848, at Concord, N. H., and received his education in the grammar and high schools of that city. After completing his education he was engaged in grocery business in Concord, and in 1866 entered the insurance business in Chicago, delivering policies for Teall & Fisher, in whose service he continued, in various capacities, until the formation of the present firm of Edward M. Teall & Co.

He is a member of the Illinois and Chicago Athletic Clubs; Sons of the American Revolution; Society of Colonial Wars, and Sons of New Hampshire.

CHARLES H. HARRADEN,

Of the Firm of Harraden & Letterman.

Chas. H. Harraden was born in Buffalo, New York, way back in the early fifties. He received his education in the public schools of that city, afterward graduating with high honors in the University of New York. He studied Law for three years in the office of Milo A. Whitney, Esq., Buffalo, New York. In 1873 he went to Texas with the view of associating himself in the practice of Law with the office of the late Gov. Throckmorton. Owing to ill-health, and in order to recuperate, he joined the Engineering Corps of the Texas Pacific R. R., remaining with them until 1878, when he returned East and was married. In 1880 he located in Chicago and entered into the employ of the Royal Insurance Company of England. In September, 1883, he transferred to the Local Office of the Hamburg-Bremen Insurance Company of Germany, remaining with this Company until 1890, when he was appointed Resident Secretary of the Prudential Fire Insurance Company of Boston, Mass., was also appointed State Agent for Illinois for the St. Paul German Accident Insurance Company, and has been prominently identified with the Underwriting Fraternity in Chicago. Mr. Harraden is a thorough, practical Underwriter, conscientious and painstaking, and one of the best versed men in Insurance laws in the State. He is a prominent member of the Royal Arcanum, Lincoln Club and several other Societies.

GEORGE M. HARVEY,

Of the Firm of George M. Harvey & Co.

George M. Harvey was born at Niagara-on-the-Lake, Canada, April 28th, 1848, and was educated at Phillips Grammar School, Niagara, Canada. He entered the Insurance business in 1864, at Buffalo, N. Y., with the firm of Rounds & Hall, where he remained five years, resigning to come to Chicago and enter the employ of S. M. Moore & Co., and later was with McCormick Bros. & Findlay, and now of the firm of George M. Harvey & Co.

Mr. Harvey was married October 19th, 1886, at Chicago, to Miss Lucy Dale Halsted, and has three children. He is a member of the Chicago Athletic and North Shore Clubs.

SEBASTIAN A. HARVEY,

Of the Firm of Darlington, Harvey & Co., Local Agents.

Sebastian A. Harvey was born in Canada, July 13th, 1846. He came to Chicago, May, 1864, and in June of the same year engaged in the business of insurance in the office of Holmes & Bro., located at the northeast corner of Clark and South Water Streets. In September, 1872, became connected with the office of Geo. C. Clarke & Co., becoming a partner January, 1881, the style of the firm changing after the death of the senior member, which occurred April, 1887, to Darlington, Harvey & Co.

LOUIS HASBROUCK,

Of the Firm of Hopkins & Hasbrouck, Local Agents.

Louis Hasbrouck was born at Alligerville, Ulster County, New York, on the 24th of March, 1856, the town being named after his grandfather. He was educated in the Public Schools and graduated from the Chicago High School in 1871. From February 1st, 1872, to January 1st, 1873, he was clerk in the office of the Treadway & Jewell Insurance Agency; January 1st, 1873, to February 1st, 1879, he was an Insurance broker, and from February 1st, 1879, he has been junior partner of the firm of Hopkins & Hasbrouck.

On the 20th of April, 1880, he was married to Miss Irene Warner, and has one boy. He is a member of the Chicago Athletic Club, Sons of New York and Royal Arcanum.

WILLIAM JEROME HEMSTREET,

Of the Firm of W. J. Hemstreet & Co., Local Agents.

William J. Hemstreet was born in the town of Lyons, Wayne County, N. Y., May 1, 1833. He received his early education in Albion Academy, Albion, N. Y., and graduated from Union High School, Lockport, N. Y.

After leaving school he worked on a farm and in 1849 went to sea on a whaling voyage. In December of that year he was, with his boat's crew, capsized by a sperm whale, which they afterward killed. Returning home from sea in 1851, he went to learn the machinist trade at Lockport, N. Y.

Mr. Hemstreet was married January 1st, 1854, at Buffalo, N. Y., to Miss Emeline A. Rapp, and has four children, two sons and two daughters. Engaged in farming from 1858 to 1861. In 1860 he voted for Lincoln and said if there was to be a war he would go. He enlisted as a private in 1861 in the 104th N. Y. S. V., and was promoted to second lieutenant in that regiment by Gov. Morgan, and in 1864 was promoted to first lieutenant, 179th N. Y. S. V., and served there until the close of the war. He was at one time the only commissioned officer with his regiment and was in command of the regiment for some time, and while in command was wounded by the fragment of a shell.

He came to Chicago at the close of the war and entered the Insurance business in 1867. He is a member of Gen. Geo. H. Thomas Post No. 5, G. A. R., Department of Illinois; Western Society of the Army of the Potomac; Illinois Commandery of Military Order of the Royal Legion; a life member of Cleveland Lodge; Washington Chapter; Siloam Council; Chicago Commandery K. T. and Oriental Consistory. A Noble of the Mystic Shrine; Member of the Society of the Sons of New York; Highland Park Club.

FRANK E. HEMSTREET

Of the Firm of W. J. Hemstreet & Co., Local Agents.

Frank E. Hemstreet was born at Lockport, Niagara County, N. Y., on the 5th of March, 1856. He removed with his parents to Chicago in 1865, and received his education in the public schools of that city. In 1871 he entered the Fire Insurance business at Chicago, continuing to follow the same profession up to the present time.

Mr. Hemstreet was married at Chicago in 1881 to Miss Caroline S. Rohde and has four children. He is a member of the Masonic Lodge, Council, Chapter and Commandery, and Ex-Captain Co. D., 1st Infantry, I. N. G.

WILLIS SCOVILLE HERRICK,

Of the Firm of R. S. Critchell & Co.

Willis Scoville Herrick was born at Oak Park, Illinois, on the 5th of September, 1865, was educated in the public schools of that place, and graduated from the High School in June, 1883, going at once into the employ of R. S. Critchell & Company, Local Agents at Chicago. This is the only office in which he has ever been employed. He was admitted to the firm in September, 1889, and now is general office man for the Local Department.

Mr. Herrick was married at Oak Park in 1886, to Miss Jewell, and has one child.

FRANK FARNSWORTH HOLMES,

Fire Insurance Agent.

Frank Farnsworth Holmes is the third son of S. R. Holmes and Rosette Farnsworth, who are descendants of the early colonists who settled in Massachusetts about 1632.

After attending the Public Schools of his native city, Warsaw, Illinois, he entered Knox College, Galesburg, Ill., graduating in 1880. He naturally adopted the profession of fire insurance, as his father and three uncles were in that line of business, and four of his brothers are, or have been engaged in the same.

Mr. Holmes has had a general experience in fire underwriting, serving as cashier, daily report examiner, correspondent, special agent and adjuster. The local agency of Frank F. Holmes & Co., was established in 1887 and has been continued since that time at 296 La Salle Street.

In 1886 he married Miss Emma A. Lewis of Lawrence, Kansas, whose mother had been the childhood friend of Mr. Holmes' father and mother in the academy village of Bakersfield, Vt.

Mr. Holmes has taken an active interest in municipal reforms, serving for one year on the first civil service examining board provided for under the city ordinances, representing the Chicago Fire Underwriters' Association on the Board of Examiners for the Chicago Building Department. He was one of the organizers of the Menoken Club, serving as trustee and treasurer since the inception of that popular and influential club, which has a large membership and owns its own grounds and building.

(281)

CHARLES RANKINS HOPKINS,
Of the Firm of Hopkins & Hasbrouck, Local Agents.

Charles R. Hopkins was born in Racine, Ohio, July 29th, 1842, and received his education at the Ohio University.

Mr. Hopkins first engaged in business in the employ of the United States government in the transportation of troops on the Mississippi River. He entered the Insurance business at Springfield, Ohio, in 1867.

Mr. Hopkins' grandfather, on his father's side, was a soldier in the War of 1812, and one of the first settlers in the State of Ohio, having assisted in the construction of Fort Harrner, at the mouth of the Muskingum River.

In 1867, at Beverly, Ohio, Mr. Hopkins married Miss Mildred A. Whissan and has one child.

He is a Mason and Knight Templar.

(282)

JAMES S. HUBBARD,

Of the Firm of Moore & Janos. Local Agents.

James S. Hubbard was born at Minaville, Montgomery County, New York, October 1st, 1845, and was educated in the Common Schools.

For some years he was engaged in railroad business at Sandusky, Cincinnati and Cleveland, and in June, 1869, entered the Insurance office of S. M. Moore & Co., at 49 La Salle Street, Chicago.

June 29th, 1871, he was married at Xenia, Ohio, to Miss Anna E. Thayer, and has two boys living.

CARL HUNCKE,

Manager, Chicago City Department of the Germania Fire Insurance Company of New York.

Carl Huncke was born on the 16th of May, 1851, at Detmold, Germany, being educated in a German college. He entered the mercantile business in Germany, and after coming to this country was surveyor and draughtsman with Samuel S. Greeley in Chicago. In 1876 he became connected with the Traders' Insurance Company of Chicago, and later was appointed manager of the Chicago branch of the Germania Fire Insurance Company of New York.

Mr. Huncke was married September 12th, 1877, in Mankato, Minn., to Miss Rosa M. Rockey. He is a member of the Germania Club and the Chicago Turn-Gemeinde.

JOHN J. JANES,

Of the Firm of Moore & Janes.

John J. Janes was born at Lansingburgh, New York, on the 10th of January, 1833, and was educated in the Common Schools of Troy, New York. His ancestors on both sides came to America in 1635, and settled in Connecticut, afterwards removing to Columbia County, New York. As a rule they were farmers, though some filled important offices, both civil and military.

Mr. Janes entered the Insurance business at Chicago, Ill., in 1864, and has been a member of the firm of S. M. Moore & Co., and Moore & Janes since 1868. He is a member of the Chicago Club and was its first Secretary, and subsequently for several years Secretary and Treasurer. He is also a member of the Commercial Club, a member of its Executive Committee, and has been Secretary of the Club for twelve years.

CHARLES P. JENNINGS

Of the Firm of Webster, Wiley & Co., Local Agents.

Charles P. Jennings was born at Dubuque, Iowa, February 19th, 1858, came to Chicago in 1865, receiving his education in the Public Schools of Hyde Park, Chicago. After leaving school he was engaged in the hardware business, entering Insurance in November, 1878, with E. E. Ryan & Co., 210 La Salle Street, Chicago, and remaining in the same business up to the present time with few changes.

He was married at Hyde Park, Chicago, September 8th, 1878, to Miss M. H. Garrigau, and has three children.

ALEXANDER D. KENNEDY,

Of the Firm of A. D. Kennedy & Co., Local Agents.

Alexander D. Kennedy was born in Kendall County, Illinois, on the 24th day of March, 1842. He received his education in the Public Schools of Chicago, and in May, 1862, entered the employ of J. K. Murphy, then local agent of the Peoria Marine & Fire Insurance Co. From an office boy he worked himself up to Cashier and Manager, and in the spring of 1866 succeeded to the appointment of agent for the same Company, doing business under the firm name of Kennedy & Williams until 1868, when the firm retired from business. Mr. Kennedy then received an appointment in the Grain Inspection Department of the State of Illinois, remaining there until 1871, when he re-entered the Insurance business as Policy Clerk and Manager of the Underwriting Department for the firm of E. E. Ryan & Co. In 1876 he was given an interest in the business, the firm continuing under the same name and consisting of Edmund E. Ryan, Holger de Roode and himself. Mr. Ryan died in 1882 and a new partnership was formed, doing business under the name of Kennedy & De Roode until 1886, when a dissolution of the firm occurred and the present firm of A. D. Kennedy & Co. was established.

In November, 1869, Mr. Kennedy was married to Miss Lizzie Elliott, and is the happy father of six children, three girls and three boys.

(287)

NATHAN KLEE,

Of the Firm of Edwards, Morse & Klee, Local Agents.

Nathan Klee was born in Grebenstein, Germany, August 4th, 1870. Coming to America in his boyhood he received his education in the Public Schools of Chicago. In March, 1885, he entered the Insurance business in the office of A. R. Edwards, later forming the firm of Edwards, Morse & Klee, Local Agents, at Chicago.

LOUIS O. KOHTZ,

Assistant General Agent. Aetna Insurance Company for Cook County, Illinois.

Louis O. Kohtz was born in Saxony, Germany, July 28th, 1844. He received his primary education in Germany, and coming to America in 1857, completed it in the schools of St. Louis, Mo. He served in the United States Army as a private in Co. F, Sixteenth Wisconsin Volunteers, and was detailed for special service in the Adjutant General's Office of the Seventeenth Army Corps at Vicksburg, Miss., where he served until the close of the war, when he entered the U. S. Quartermaster's Department at Fort Morgan, Colo., remaining there until 1866. In 1868 he entered the Aetna Insurance Company's Local office at Chicago, Ill.

Mr. Kohtz is a member of the Board of Education of the City of Chicago, and of the Geo. H. Thomas Post. G. A. R. He was married at Chicago, and has four children.

WILLIAM GEORGE LEMAY,

Of the Firm of A. D. Kennedy & Co., Local Agents.

William George Lemay was born at London, England, September 13th, 1851, and received his education in a private academy of that place. He commenced his business career in a book publishing establishment and entered the Insurance business in 1884, with A. D. Kennedy, with which firm he has remained up to the present time.

Mr. Lemay was married at Chicago in 1881. He is a member of the Chicago Commandery, K. T., the Royal Arcanum, the National Union and the Menoken Club.

EDMUND R. LETTERMAN,

Of the Firm of Harraden & Letterman, Local Agents.

Edmund R. Letterman was born at Pekin, Illinois, September 24th, 1863, of German descent, and was educated in the High School of that place. He came to Chicago in July, 1882, and entered the employ of the Fireman's Insurance Company of Chicago, was made Assistant Secretary in 1890, and Acting Secretary in 1891. He resigned in June, 1892, and became Manager of the Local Department of the Oakland Home Insurance Company of California, remaining with that company until it re-insured in January, 1894. He entered the firm of C. H. Harraden & Co., in August, 1894, changing firm name to Harraden & Letterman.

ISAAC JOHN LEWIS,

Local Agent.

Isaac John Lewis was born in Mahaska County, Iowa, June 9th, 1845, and received a public school education at Burlington, Iowa, and Cleveland, Ohio. In 1862 he entered the insurance business at Cleveland as office boy with May & Coe, Insurance Agents. In October, 1866, he came to Chicago as the representative of the Cleveland Insurance Company and Commercial Mutual Insurance Company of Cleveland, Ohio, and engaged in the local insurance business. He has resided in Chicago ever since, being still engaged in the same business.

June 18th, 1867, he was married at Cleveland, Ohio, to Miss Annie F. Loud. He is a member of Cleveland Lodge No. 211, A. F. and A. M., Underwriters' Council, Chicago Athletic and Washington Park Clubs.

LEO A. LOEB,

Of the Firm of A. Loeb, Son & Co.

Leo A. Loeb was born in Memphis, Tenn., June 20th, 1867. He was educated in the Public Schools of Chicago and embarked in the employ of Adolph Loeb, his father, in the year 1880. Was made a member of the firm January 1st, 1888, and thus has been in the "profession" his entire life. Besides his identification with this firm, he is President of the Traders' Building and Loan Association. Assistant Secretary of the Commercial Loan and Building Association, and a Director in the Aetna Building and Loan Association. He is a member of the Standard Club and is actively associated with many public benevolent institutions and charities.

JACOB M. LOEB,

Of the Firm of Loeb & Coffey, Local Agents.

Jacob M. Loeb is a Chicago boy, born September 17th, 1874, and is proud of the fact of being one of the youngest agents in Chicago.

He was educated in the Chicago public schools, and took to Insurance naturally. His relatives are engaged in real estate and mortgage loan business, and Mr. Loeb handles all their insurance for them. Loeb & Coffee are doing to-day perhaps the largest preferred business of any firm in the city, controlling large lines of several of the biggest real estate offices, and principally on dwelling house property. Mr. Loeb is well and favorabl known among the insurance fraternity, is in close touch with the boys, among whom he has a peck of nicknames. He is a hard worker, early and late, and has the reputation of securing the risk when he goes for it. In fact, to make a short cut of the whole business, "Jake's" a "hustler," and a Chicago one at that.

JAMES I. LOEB,

Of the Firm of Niblock & Loob.

James I. Loeb was born in Cincinnati, Ohio, on the 7th of January, 1874; was educated in the Grammar and High Schools; then entered the furniture business at Kansas City; came to Chicago in the spring of 1891, entering the employ of A. Loeb & Son (Mr. Adolph Loeb being his uncle); remained there until May, 1895, when he formed a partnership with H. C. Niblock, under the firm name of Niblock & Loeb, doing general brokerage business.

Mr. Loeb is a Mason and member of the Marquette Club, Chicago.

EDSON W. LYMAN,

Of the Firm of Straight & Lyman, District Managers.

Edson W. Lyman is a native of New York, and was born in the County of Cattaraugus, near the village of Farmersville. While yet a lad he removed with his parents, who were farmers, to Illinois, locating in Whiteside County in 1857. He obtained his education at the district school, Mt. Carroll Seminary, then an institution of learning for both sexes, and at the University of Michigan. He graduated from the law department of the latter institution and was admitted to practice by the Supreme Court of Illinois, sitting at Ottawa, and in the year 1865 opened an office at Pontiac, Livingston County.

He was also appointed Local Agent of the Aetna Insurance Company of Hartford, and afterwards Special Agent, under the late General Agent, J. B. Bennett, for several counties in the central portion of the State.

Opportunities for more extended field work continued to present themselves and caused his removal to Rockford. He became Special Agent of the Reaper City Insurance Company of Rockford for a large portion of the West. After the retirement of that company he was appointed Special Agent of the Niagara Fire Insurance Company of New York, for Illinois and Wisconsin.

In the spring of 1875 he resigned his field position with the Niagara Fire Insurance Company and entered into partnership with Mr. H. J. Straight, under the firm name of Straight & Lyman, with offices at that time at 150 La Salle Street, Chicago. They became General Agents for the Western States of the New York Alliance, and for several years he continued active in the management of that combination and until the condition of one of the companies forming it necessitated its discontinuance. His firm are at present District Managers of the Sun Insurance Company of London, for Cook County, and also represent the Standard Fire Insurance Company of Trenton, N. J., and the Manchester Fire Assurance Company of England.

Mr. Lyman was a soldier in the late war. Early in 1862 he enlisted in the Seventy-Fifth Regiment of Illinois Volunteers, was made a sergeant and served with the regiment until so severely wounded at the Battle of Perryville as to require his discharge from further military duty. He is one of the original members of the Union League Club and is also connected with several other local organizations.

GEORGE M. LYON,

Of the Firm of Ducat & Lyon, Local Managers.

Mr. George M. Lyon was born at Bedford, Pennsylvania, on the 18th of May, 1841, and was educated in private academies in Pennsylvania. His father was a very prominent attorney in Pennsylvania and had an extensive practice in Bedford, Blair, Somerset, Fulton, Franklin and Adams County, Pennsylvania, as well as before the Supreme Court of that State, at the same time as Hon. Jeremiah S. Black, Thaddeus Stevens, Chief Justices Thompson and Chambers, and with other leading attorneys of that section, with all of whom he was often associated in the same courts, and he was the Whig candidate to succeed Jeremiah S. Black, as President Judge of the district. His ancestors and family connections have been prominently identified with the history of Pennsylvania from before the Revolution until the present time.

Mr. Lyon taught school in Bedford County from 1857 to 1858 and on May 1st, 1859, entered the New York City office of the Home Insurance Company, where he was a clerk until 1867, at which time he was then made Assistant Secretary of the Company and remained so until October, 1873, when he came to Chicago and opened partnership with General A. C. Ducat, under the firm name of Ducat & Lyon, who are now in the General Local Agency business for Chicago, and who were managers of the Western Department of the Home Insurance Company of New York until its transfer to New York in October, 1893.

HENRY WATERS MAGILL,

District Manager Phoenix Insurance Company of Hartford, Conn.

Henry Waters Magill was born in the city of Cincinnati, Ohio, on the 11th day of July, 1863, being the eldest son of H. M. Magill of Cincinnati, General Agent of the Western and Southern Department of the Phoenix Insurance Company of Hartford, Conn. He was educated in public and private schools in Avondale and Cincinnati, and was graduated from Harvard University, Cambridge, Mass., in 1886. He began business as a young man in the General Agency office of the Phoenix, and was appointed Special Agent of that Company for Michigan the latter part of 1886. In September, 1888, he became a member of the firm of Ayars & Magill, having charge of Chicago and Cook County. Upon the death of Captain Ayars in August, 1893, he succeeded to the firm.

Mr. Magill is a member of the Fire Underwriters' Association of the Northwest, Avon Lodge, F. and A. M., No. 542, Avondale, Ohio; Chicago Athletic Association, University Club of Chicago, and Harvard Alumni Association.

WILLIAM C. MAGILL.

Of the Firm of W. G. Magill & Co., Local Agents.

William Charles Magill was born at Buffalo, N. Y., June 11th, 1856, and was about four years old when his family came to Chicago. He was educated at the Skinner School, of Chicago, afterward taking a course at Immanuel Hall, a military school at Ravenswood.

Leaving school at the age of seventeen he entered his father's office as clerk and cashier. He was subsequently connected with other commission houses, dealing "on 'change," and in April, 1874, became the representative on the Board of Trade of the Insurance firm of George C. Clark & Co. He continued to be Solicitor and Manager of the Marine Department of this concern for some years. Since 1880 he has given exclusive attention to fire underwriting, being successively a member of the firms of Magill & Nichols, Geo. W. Montgomery & Co., and Magill & Chamberlin, the last-named firm having been organized October 1st, 1889, and continuing until October 1st, 1895, at which time the firm was dissolved by mutual consent, the present firm of Wm. C. Magill & Co. succeeding.

On the 12th of November, 1873, Mr. Magill was married to Miss Mary C. Montgomery, a daughter of Robert Montgomery, a prominent shipper and vessel-owner of Buffalo, N. Y. His residence for the past twenty years has been in the beautiful suburban town of Evanston, where he for four years served as a town trustee. He is prominently identified with the Masonic Order, holding membership with the Evans Lodge, Evanston Commandery, Oriental Consistory and Medinah Temple. At different times he has been actively associated with several other social and fraternal organizations, including the Evanston Club and the Evanston Boat Club. Fidelity to all trusts has always been his motto. Since his twenty-second year he has been an active worker in the Republican Party.

KOSSUTH MARKS,

Of the Firm of R. S. Critchell & Co., Local Agents.

Kossuth Marks was born in Chicago and educated in the schools of his native city. After finishing his education, he entered the insurance office of W. H. Cunningham & Co., and soon rose to a position of trust. In 1889 he became a member of the firm of R. S. Critchell & Co. He is a member of the Chicago Athletic Association and other organizations.

WILLIAM DIXON MARSH,

Of the Firm of Fred S. James & Co., Local Agents.

William Dixon Marsh was born at Ellington, Conn., on the 7th of February, 1840; was educated at Williston Seminary, East Hampton, Mass., and entered the Fire Insurance business at Chicago in 1869. After the fire of 1871, Mr. Marsh was for five years connected with the agency of Davis & ReQua, as Solicitor. In July, 1876, he entered into partnership with Henry H. Brown, the firm name being Brown & Marsh, at 158 La Salle Street, which continued for two years, when Mr. Marsh retired to accept an offer from Fred S. James, to become his partner, the firm being then made Fred S. James & Co. The firm is still in business at 174 La Salle Street, where Mr. Marsh is an active partner.

Mr. Marsh was married in 1864, at Chicago, to Josephine E. Thayer; had two children, and in 1883, at Madison, Wis., to Lora E. Campbell, and had one child.

He is a trustee of the Illinois College of Jacksonville, Ill., a director of the Chicago City Missionary Society, a member of the Union League Club, and one of the charter members of the New England Society.

JOHN MOFFAT MATHER,

Of the Firm of Straight & Lyman, District Managers.

John Moffat Mather is a native of Indiana, having been born at Lawrenceburg, in that State, May 26th, 1862. He received his education in the Grammar and High Schools of Indianapolis, coming to Illinois in 1879. He worked for a short time in the grocery business, but in May, 1880, he entered the Insurance office of Straight & Lyman as clerk, and occupied various responsible positions. On Jan. 1st, 1893, he was given charge of the office force and admitted to an interest in the firm.

In July, 1886, he was married to Margaret F. Clark of this city; two little girls brighten their home. Mr. Mather is thoroughly domestic in his tastes; his chief delight after the day's work is with his family and books.

BAVIER C. MILLER,

Of the Firm of Granger Smith, Miller & Co., Local Agents.

Bavier C. Miller was born at Claverack, Columbia County, New York, on the eighth day of October, 1858, removing to Chicago at an early age, and receiving his education in the Public Schools of that city. The first business he engaged in was Fire Insurance, which he entered in 1873 with the firm of Teall & Fisher, at Chicago, Illinois.

Mr. Miller was married at Chicago in 1880, to Miss Jennie B. Dole and has two children. He is a member of several clubs and organizations in Chicago, among which are the Chicago Athletic Association and Menoken Clubs and the Royal Arcanum (Garden City Council), Sons of New York and others.

Mr. Miller has been associated with the firm of Granger Smith, Miller & Co., for over twenty years.

GEORGE W. MONTGOMERY,

Of the Firm of George Montgomery & Co., Local Agents.

George W. Montgomery is a native of Genessee County, New York, where his boyhood days were spent until seventeen years of age, when he came to Chicago and took the position of bookkeeper in the wholesale drug house of J. H. Reed & Co. Two years later he went with the firm of A. E. Kent & Co., packers, where he remained until he entered the Army, in 1862, as a member of the celebrated Mercantile Battery of Chicago. Owing to exposure and rough usage at the siege of Vicksburg his health became impaired and he was obliged to return home, having received his honorable discharge in March, 1863. Bad health prevented his engaging in any business until 1864, when he was appointed cashier of the Internal Revenue office at Chicago. A year later he identified himself with the wholesale dry goods house of D. H. King & Co., and remained there until that firm retired from business. In 1869 he became a partner with O. W. Barrett in the Fire Insurance business. This partnership continued until 1873, when the connection was severed and another formed with Abram Williams, under the firm name of Williams & Montgomery. A year later Mr. Williams retired and Mr. Montgomery continued the local agency on his own account. This he has conducted ever since, representing the interests of several prominent companies in the city of Chicago acceptably and profitably to all concerned.

Mr. Montgomery was Vice-President of the Underwriters' Exchange of this city in 1884, and President in 1885. He was one of the founders of the Chicago Athenaeum and a member of the first board of directors of that institution. He is a prominent member of the Chicago Club, and was its Secretary and Treasurer in 1883.

JAMES H. MOORE,

Of the Firm of Moore & Janes, Local Agents.

James H. Moore was born in Windham, N. H., July 4th, 1840, where he spent his boyhood, attending the Public Schools, and later, Chester Academy. When sixteen, like many another of New Hampshire's sons, he left the rugged granite hills for the broad prairies of the West, locating at Mendota, Illinois. In 1859 he went to Elgin, Illinois, and from that time until July, 1861, was employed in the Elgin Bank, when he resigned to enlist as a soldier in the War of the Rebellion. He joined the Thirty-sixth Regiment of Illinois Infantry, and served until September, 1863. Upon his return from the army he removed to Chicago, where he has since resided. He at that time entered the office of L. D. Olmsted & Co., with which he has been connected ever since; the firm name having changed in the meantime to S. M. Moore & Co., and later, to its present style of Moore & Janes. The Hartford Fire and Mr. Moore entered Olmsted & Co.'s at about the same time and neither one has any reason to regret the step then taken. Together they have watched the development of the city by the unsalted sea, and both have contributed their share to its present greatness. Mr. Moore has been connected with every underwriters' organization which has existed in Chicago, and for two years has served as President of the Chicago Fire Underwriters' Association, proving himself a man of fine executive ability. Possessed of the true New England spirit, Mr. Moore has made it his aim to excel in his line, and the result of that determination is, that the agency of Moore & Janes is second to none in Chicago.

DAVID SELDEN MUNGER,

Of the Firm of Munger, Ebbert & Co.

David S. Munger was born in Bainbridge, Chenango County, New York, December 25, 1824. He was about ten years old when the family moved to Homer, N. Y., where he attended the old Homer Academy, completing the course at the age of twenty years. About 1850 he went to Binghamton, N. Y., and engaged in mercantile business; later he was similarly occupied at Pottersville, N. Y. In 1859 he came west and engaged in farming at Merton, Wis. Five years later he became a resident of Chicago, which city has since been his home. His first business venture here was in the capacity of solicitor for the Mutual Life Insurance Company of New York. Up to the time of the great fire he divided his attention between Fire and Life Insurance, but since 1871 has given his exclusive attention to Fire Underwriting.

In 1872 he was appointed Agent of the Franklin Fire Insurance Company of Boston, under the firm name of D. S. Munger & Company. In 1877 he was made Agent of the New York Underwriters' Agency of New York. In 1880 F. B. Hosmer came into the firm, bringing the Scottish Union and National Insurance Company into the Agency. In 1887 W. H. Ebbert became a member of the above firm. In January, 1893, the firm name was changed to Munger, Ebbert & Co. J. W. Vokoun was made a member of the firm in January, 1894.

They have the management for Cook County of the two last mentioned companies, together with the Hanover Fire Insurance Company of New York, and are recognized as conservative and successful business men.

(306)

JOHN NAGHTEN,

Of the Firm of John Naghten & Co., Local Agents.

John Naghten was born in Ireland, coming to this country when a young man. He commenced his insurance experience in 1857 in the insurance office of Wm. H. Smith. With the organization of the Merchants' Insurance Company, May, 1863, he became associated with, and shortly afterwards was appointed assistant secretary of that company, which position he filled up to the time of the great fire of '71. Shortly after the fire the Traders' Insurance Company was re-organized, Mr. Naghten being appointed assistant secretary of the company, continuing in that position until 1873, when the co-partnership of Rollo, Naghten & Co. was formed. In 1877 he associated with him his son, M. J. Naghten, forming the partnership of John Naghten & Co., of which firm he is now the senior member.

Mr. Naghten is one of the oldest insurance men in the city of Chicago, having had a continuous experience of over thirty-eight years. During part of this time he was the General Agent of several companies, but of late years has confined himself to doing local business.

MICHAEL J. NAGHTEN,

Of the Firm of John Naghten & Co., Local Agents.

Michael J. Naghten was born in the State of Pennsylvania. He attended the public schools for a time and completed his education in St. Ignatius College of Chicago.

June, 1874, he commenced his insurance career with the firm of Rollo, Naghten & Co.

Mr. Naghten is one of the organizers of the Metropolitan Insurance Company of Chicago, and at the present time holds the position of secretary for the same company.

HARRY C. NIBLOCK,

Of the Firm of Niblock & Loob.

Harry C. Niblock was born at Youngstown, Ohio, May 24th, 1863, receiving his education in the public schools. He entered Insurance at Indianapolis, Indiana, in 1879, continuing in the same profession up to the present time.

Mr. Niblock was married June 1st, 1886, at Sioux City, Iowa, to Miss Abbie E. Goewey. He is a member of the Lincoln Park Commandery, K. T.; Oriental Consistory, S. P. R. S., 32 degree Medinah Temple, A. A. O. N. S. and Marquette Club.

JOSEPH S. PHILLIPS,

Of the Firm of Fred S. James & Co., Local Agents.

Joseph S. Phillips was born in Hamburg, Germany, on the 26th of June, 1839, and was educated in the public schools. Served in the United States army during the war, after which he was engaged in mercantile business, and entered the Insurance business in September, 1873. He has been connected with Fred S. James & Co. since May, 1874.

Mr. Phillips was married on the 18th of September, 1870, at Chicago, to Miss Sarah Jacoby, and has six children. He is identified with several organizations in Chicago, among them being the Masons, Grand Army of the Republic (U. S. Grant, No. 28, Department Illinois), and the Western Society of the Army of the Potomac.

STEPHEN F. RE QUA,

Of the Firm of Davis & ReQua. Local Agents.

Stephen F. ReQua was born at Kendall, Orleans County, N. Y., on the 16th of October, 1836, of French descent, his ancestors being Huguenots who came to this country to escape persecution in France.

The ReQua family were largely represented in the Revolutionary War. In 1894 a monument was erected in the old Dutch churchyard at Tarrytown, New York, to the Revolutionary heroes buried there. On the marble seventy-one names are inscribed, eleven of which are ReQua, which would seem to show a pretty strong strain of fighting, patriotic blood.

Mr. ReQua's early life was spent on his father's farm, and he received his education in the common schools and at Genessee College, Lima, New York. He came to Chicago in 1864 and engaged in the Insurance business, continuing in the same ever since.

CHARLES M. ROGERS,

General Agent, American Central and New Hampshire Fire Insurance Companies for Cook County, Illinois.

Charles M. Rogers was born April 30th, 1856, at Philadelphia, Penn. His father was an officer in the Army and contracted a disease which eventually killed him. Mr. Rogers was compelled to leave school when thirteen years old and enter a dry goods store at a salary of $2 per week, helping with his brother (who was two years older than himself), to support his widowed mother and three sisters. His experience in the Insurance business, which he became connected with in 1872, has been from office boy and messenger to his present position, without money or influence, simply strict attention to business and plenty of hard work.

Mr. Rogers was married at Chicago, Ill., to Miss Hattie L. Merchant, and has two children, a son and daughter. He is a member of the Menoken Club of Chicago, Evanston Boat Club, Royal Arcanum, Royal League and National Union.

FRANK P. SHELDON,

Of the Firm of Hammond, Fry & Sheldon, Local Agents.

Frank P. Sheldon was born in New York City, December 31, 1853. He moved to Chicago with his parents in 1856, and with the exception of four years which he spent in Jersey City, has resided in this city. In September, 1871, he entered the office of the Republic Fire Insurance Company as clerk; later, was with the firm of Bowmar & Waller. In 1875, he entered the employ of L. D. Hammond, becoming a partner in the firm of Hammond & Fry, in 1887.

JOHN ELDON SHEPHERD,

Assistant Superintendent Cook County Department Manchester Fire Assurance Company.

John E. Shepherd was born at Macon City, Mo., on the 24th of May, 1871. He was educated in the Common Schools of Chicago, West Side High School, Lake Forest University and University of Tennessee.

His family are among the oldest in America, both his father's and mother's people having settled in Jamestown, Va., in the early part of the seventeenth century. Several members of the family bore themselves with honor during the Revolutionary, Mexican and Civil Wars; and in the field of politics they also distinguished themselves, one rising to the dignity of Vice-President of the United States and another being twice Governor of Missouri.

Mr. Shepherd made his first business venture in 1891 at Chicago, as Cashier of the Liberty Insurance Company, and later was engaged in Real Estate and Insurance, following the profession for some time at Oklahoma City, Oklahoma Territory. In the spring of 1895 he sold out his business and became connected with the Manchester Fire Assurance Company in the capacity of Assistant Superintendent of the Cook County Department.

Mr. Shepherd is a member of the Signa Alpha Epsilon College Fraternity. He was married at Chicago in 1893 to Miss Thyra Richardson, and has one son.

GRANGER SMITH,

Of the Firm of Granger Smith, Miller & Co., Local Agents.

Granger Smith was born at Buffalo, New York, March 19th, 1849. His father's family were Quakers of New Bedford, Mass., and his mother's family (Granger) who came from Connecticut, were scions of the early wars and very conspicuously identified with the early history of Buffalo. From fourteen to twenty-one, Mr. Smith was in the employ of a large commission firm in Buffalo, and from office boy rose to be head of the office. He comes of an insurance family, his father having represented the old Hartford Companies in Buffalo, writing policies over fifty years ago. All his four brothers were in the Aetna General Agency at Cincinnati, at the time Mr. Smith was about eleven years of age, being the youngest of the family. He served in the New York State Militia, in crack Company D, Seventy-fourth Regiment, and also in the Volunteer Fire Department, being a member of the "Taylor Hose, No. 1," an organization well known for its high social status, as well as for its usefulness before the advent of the Paid Department in Buffalo. He removed to Chicago in 1873 and established his agency that year and is proud of the fact that thus far no company has ever left the agency for another. Mr. Smith is a man of conservative ideas and habits and has a high sense of duty and integrity and is especially endeared to his junior partners, who have all been boys in the office and are like a happy family together, and always thoughtful for the interests of each other as well as their clients. Mr. Smith was married in 1870 to Miss Mary B. Pitts. Is one of the oldest members of the Union League Club, and is also a member of the Royal Arcanum, the Chicago Athletic Association, Sons of the American Revolution, Sons of New York, and other social organizations. He owns considerable property in Chicago and Waukegan.

WILLIAM E. SPANGENBERG,

Manager for Cook County of the German Insurance Company of Freeport, Ill., and the Milwaukee Mechanics' Insurance Company of Milwaukee, Wis.

William E. Spangenberg was born at Bunker Hill, Illinois, in the early sixties, of American-German parents. After finishing the public schools he passed three years in Bunker Hill Academy. He began business in his father's local agencies in Bunker Hill, and in October, 1884, entered the office of A. D. Kennedy in Chicago, as office boy, and by hard work and strict attention worked himself up, and when the branch office of the German and Milwaukee Mechanics' was opened in May, 1889, went with these companies and took position as counter clerk. In January, 1891, was taken in as partner with Simeon Schupp, and served so faithfully that on the death of Mr. Schupp, in December, 1893, was made manager of these two well-known companies, the German Insurance Company of Freeport, Illinois, and the Milwaukee Mechanics' Insurance Company, of Milwaukee, Wisconsin, for the city of Chicago and Cook County. Mr. Spangenberg is a member of Underwriters' Council, National Union and also Royal Arcanum.

He was married April 7th, 1891, to Miss Flora J. Schupp.

(316)

WILLIAM THOMPSON STEWARD,

Of the Firm of Steward, French & Co., Local Agents.

William Thompson Steward was born in the State of Ohio in 1853, and was educated in the common schools of Ohio and Michigan.

He commenced business as a Cashier and Accountant, and in 1885 entered the Insurance business at Chicago. He was married in Michigan in the year 1878, and has one child.

CHARLES R. STOUFFER,

Of the Firm of Thos. S. Cunningham & Co., Managers of Cook County.

Charles R. Stouffer was born at Harrisburg, Penn., on the 12th of June, 1847. He commenced business life in Chicago in 1864, with the wholesale clothing house of Wm. R. Lovejoy & Co.

In 1880 he resigned his position as bookkeeper in the Treasury Department of the Chicago & Northwestern Ry. Co. to enter the employ of Wm. H. Cunningham & Co.

HIRAM S. STRAIGHT,

Of the Firm of Straight & Lyman, District Managers.

Hiram J. Straight was born near Fredonia, Chautauqua County, New York, his father being a farmer and one of the pioneers of that county. After attending the public schools he completed his education at the Ellington Academy, and at the age of eighteen, in common with many other young men, he readily accepted the advice of Horace Greeley, his equipment seeming to be complete minus the one thousand dollars.

Coming to Illinois he located on a farm in Livingston County. The occupation of farming not proving congenial he engaged in the Fire Insurance business at Fairbury. As early as 1866 he accepted the Agency of several leading companies, including the Aetna, Hartford, Phoenix, Home of New York, and the Insurance Company of North America, and also acted as Special Agent of the Actna as well as Local. The valuable education gained during his connection with these companies was of great advantage in preparing him to successfully occupy a larger field.

Achieving reasonable success with the opportunities offered at that time and place, his ambition led him to seek wider fields, and with his native foresight, was led to believe that Chicago would soon become the metropolis of the country, and in the spring of 1874 disposed of his business at Fairbury and opened an office at 151 La Salle Street, where he began active operations. In the fall of that year he removed to 150 La Salle Street, where he remained for about sixteen years, when a larger office was found necessary and was obtained by a removal to the present commodious quarters now occupied by his firm at Nos. 200 and 202 La Salle Street.

When the Sun Insurance Office of London entered the United States Messrs. Straight & Lyman were selected from the list of applicants as their Chicago Agents and are still the representatives of that company. This firm also represents the Manchester Fire Assurance Company of England and the Standard Fire Insurance Company of Trenton, N. J., the latter being the first company to enter their agency over twenty years ago.

Mr. Straight is a member of the Chicago Board of Trade, the Stock Exchange, the Union League Club of Chicago, the Chicago Art Institute, the Society of the Sons of New York, and the Prairie Club of Oak Park, and has been a liberal contributor to the Oak Park Library Association, known as the Scoville Institute.

JOHN T. SWEETLAND,

Of the Firm of D. T. Devin & Co., Local Agents.

John T. Sweetland was born at Cazenovia, Madison County, New York, August 25th, 1849, and was educated in Cazenovia Seminary.

Mr. Sweetland is a member of various clubs and societies, among them being the Woodlawn Park Club. He was married to Miss Mary E. Doty, April 20th, 1881, and has one son, J. T. Sweetland, Jr.

He commenced his business life in a general dry goods and country store, entering the insurance business in 1868, with the firm of Hunt & Goodwin, agents for the Aetna Insurance Company of Hartford, Conn., remaining with them nine years, then being connected with the firm of James A. Miller & Co., for eight years, resigning in 1893 to accept his present position with the firm of D. T. Devin & Co.

EDWARD M. TEALL,

Of the Firm of Edward M. Teall & Co., Local Agents.

Edward M. Teall was born at Albany, New York, July 27th, 1839, and received his primary education in private schools and afterwards became a student in Albany Academy. He was first engaged in wholesale flour and grain business at Albany, with the firm of Smyth & Gifford. March 4th, 1857, he came to Chicago and later secured employment as clerk in the Insurance office of Higginson & James. In 1862 he became one of the partners of the firm of Alfred James & Co., which firm continued to transact business for about three years. He afterwards formed a partnership with Frederick F. Fisher, a relation which continued for ten years, at the end of that period the present firm of Edward M. Teall & Co. was formed. Mr. Teall is one of the directors of the Westchester Fire Insurance Company of New York; he was Vice-President of the old Board of Underwriters; President for two years of the Chicago Underwriters' Exchange; President of the Chicago Fire Underwriters' Association for three years; and is now President of the Chicago Underwriters' Association. He is a member and officer in the Third Presbyterian Church; also a member of the Illinois Club, and Deputy Governor of the Society of Colonial Wars of the State of Illinois, which he helped to organize; and also a member of the Illinois Society of the Sons of the American Revolution.

Mr. Teall was married to Miss Katherine Mead on the 11th of June, 1862.

HERBERT J. ULLMANN,

Of the Firm of R. A. Waller & Co., Local Agents.

Herbert J. Ullmann was born on the 9th of November, 1855, at Racine, Wisconsin, and removed with his father's family to Chicago in 1860. After completing his education in the Public Schools of Chicago, he obtained a situation with the Washington Ice Company, and was afterwards engaged in the lumber business with the Ludington, Wells & Van Schaick Co.

He entered the Insurance business in 1873 as Solicitor for Dan M. Bowmar, becoming a clerk for A. G. Van Schaick in 1874 and a member of the firm of Bowmar & Ullmann in 1875; was an insurance broker from 1876 to 1885 and became a member of the firm of O. W. Barrett & Co. October 1st, 1885. Ten months after the death of Mr. O. W. Barrett (which occurred July 2d, 1893), the agency of O. W. Barrett & Co consolidated with R. A. Waller & Co., Mr. Ullmann becoming a member of the latter firm.

Mr. Ullmann served in Illinois National Guard for seven years in Company F, First Infantry, of which Company he was successively First Sergeant, Second Lieutenant, First Lieutenant and Captain. He resigned in November, 1883, and joined the Veteran Corps of the First Regiment, of which he is still a member.

April 30th, 1884, Mr. Ullmann was married at Vincennes, Ind., to Miss Clara R. Williams, who with their family of three sons now reside at Oak Park. He is a member of Chicago Athletic Association, Oak Park Club, Church Club of Chicago, Brotherhood of St. Andrew, and Veteran Corps, First Infantry Illinois National Guard.

(322)

JOSEPH J. VAN EVERY,

Of the Firm of Gowan & Van Every, Local Agents.

Joseph J. Van Every was born in Goderich, Province of Ontario, Canada, on the 21st of October, 1857, receiving his education in the Canadian public schools. He was first engaged in general merchandise business, entering the insurance field in 1875, at Chicago, Ill., with the firm of Davis & ReQua, Local Agents; remaining with them until the formation of the firm of which he is now a member.

He was married to Miss Frances M. Anderson (second daughter of Captain Andrew Anderson, formerly a prominent marine insurance man in Chicago before the great fire), on the 18th of November, 1884, and has two children.

JOHN W. VOKOUN,

Junior Member of the Firm of Munger, Ebbert & Co.

John W. Vokoun was born in Austria, February 27th, 1870, coming to Chicago when a boy and receiving his education in the public schools of that city.

In April, 1885, he entered the office of Munger, Ebbert & Co., as a clerk, and by his strict attention to duty has worked himself up to the position which he now holds in the firm.

ROBERT ALEXANDER WALLER,

Of the Firm of R. A. Waller & Co.

Robert A. Waller was born in the Blue Grass region of Kentucky in 1850. His family moved to Chicago in 1858 where Mr. Waller received his preparatory education. He was invested with high honors upon his graduation from Washington and Lee University in 1872. When he left college he entered the Insurance business as a clerk, and in the course of two years became a partner in the firm of Bowmar & Waller. In 1876 he married Miss Watson of Frankfort, Ky. Three years later, on account of Mr. Bowmar's ill health and consequent retirement, the Insurance firm was changed to R. A. Waller & Co., under which name the business is still carried on. Besides being an influential Underwriter, conducting one of the largest offices in Chicago, Mr. Waller is prominent in other departments of Chicago's busy life. He was one of the organizers and the first president of the Sheridan Drive Association; was also appointed one of the Lincoln Park Commissioners, and after the death of Mr. Goudy he was chosen President of the Board. Under his administration the Board was very active in many directions, especially in the extension of the Lake Shore Drive and the improvement of that portion of the drive between Bellevue place and the water-works. From its inception Mr. Waller was a member of the Board of Directors of the World's Columbian Exposition, and occupied responsible positions on several of its committees. He was elected Second Vice-President of the Exposition, and to his efforts much of the success of the World's Fair was due. He is now a member of the Civil Service Commission.

With the pride of a true Southerner, Mr. Waller is able to trace his ancestry through generations of one of Kentucky's best families.

Mr. Waller possesses an engaging personality and his popularity among all classes of business men is unbounded. He has large property interests, being part owner of the Ashland Block, and is also founder of one of Chicago's prettiest suburbs, Buena Park. Mr. Waller's social standing is very high. He is a member of the Iroquois, University, Chicago, Fellowship, Union, Athletic, and Union League clubs, and is connected with various other social and commercial organizations.

THOMAS HOLMES WEBSTER,
Of the Firm of Webster, Wiley & Co.

Thomas Holmes Webster was born at Leeds, England, October 29th, 1846, and came to this country in his boyhood. He was educated in the Chicago Public Schools and commenced his business career as clerk in a dry goods store, where he remained for about one year; in August, 1863, he entered the employ of the Chicago Firemen's Insurance Company, as office boy, the office being then located at the northwest corner of Lake and Clark Streets. He has resided in Chicago since 1855, a period of forty years, thirty-two of which have been continuously spent in the Insurance business. It is safe to say that no one in the profession has the confidence and esteem of his associates more fully than himself. Webster, Wiley & Co. are Cook County managers of the Lion Fire Insurance Company, of London, Eng., and General Agents for the Commerce Insurance Company, of Albany, N. Y.

September 13th, 1881, Mr. Webster was married to Miss Anna Martindale. They have had three children, two of whom are now living. He is a member of the Union League and Metropolitan Clubs and the Lexington Council of the National Union.

(326)

CHARLES PRATT WHITNEY,

Of the Firm of Granger Smith, Miller & Co., Local Agents.

Charles Pratt Whitney, member of the firm of Granger Smith, Miller & Co., Local Agents, was born at Shelburne Falls, Mass., July 14th, 1866, and was educated in the public schools of Chicago. He commenced business in 1880, in a fire insurance office at Chicago.

Mr. Whitney married Miss Grace Elizabeth Lewis in 1888 and has two children, both boys. He is Vice-President of the Chicago Athletic Club, Secretary and Treasurer of the Massachusetts Society in Chicago and is a member of the Sons of the American Revolution and other societies.

EDWARD N. WILEY,

Of the Firm of Webster, Wiley & Co.

Edward N. Wiley was born at Hartford, Conn., March 8th, 1855, of old New England stock. His ancestors, who came to this country from England about 1640, fought nobly in the Revolution for the independence of their country.

Mr. Wiley received a thorough education in the Public Schools of Hartford, which prepared him for his successful business career.

After leaving school he accepted a position in a wholesale dry goods house, resigning to enter the Insurance field July 1st, 1881, at Chicago, Ills., since which time he has been continuously in the profession, filling every position which he has held with credit to himself and his company.

May 31st, 1883, he was married at Chicago, Ill., to Miss Jennie Moore, daughter of S. M. Moore. He is a member of the Royal Arcanum, National Union, Chicago Athletic and Kenwood Clubs.

(328)

HENRY NEWTON WILLIAMS,

Of the Firm of Williams, Dana & Deems, Local Agents.

Henry Newton Williams is a native of Windham, Ohio, and was born on the 2d of October, 1845. He was educated in the common schools of Ohio and entered business at Hartford, Wisconsin, August 1st, 1865, as a local insurance agent, which position he held until October 1st, 1875. He was Special Agent for the British American and Phoenix Assurance Companies to January 1st, 1885, Secretary of the Fireman's Insurance Company, Dayton, Ohio, to April 1st, 1888, General Adjuster for the Phoenix Assurance to January 1st, 1891; General Agent for the Western Department of the Oakland Home Insurance Company of California to January 1st, 1894, and is a member of the local Agency firm of Williams, Dana & Deems at the present time.

Mr. Williams was married at Hartford, Wisconsin, July 16th, 1870, to Miss Fanny A. Murray and has one daughter. He is a member of the Chicago Whist Club and Masonic Lodge, Chapter and Commandery at Evanston, Illinois.

(329)

WILLIAM G. WOOD,

Of the Firm of W. G. Wood & Son, Local Agents.

William G. Wood was born at Fort Plain, New York, in 1824, went to Morristown, Lamoille County, Vt., when he was three years of age. His ancestors were Vermonters, and well known pioneers of the State. From his early youth, up to the age of seventeen, he worked on a farm summers, and during the entire year, with the exception of about two months of each year spent at school. Subsequently he attended the Academies at Johnson and Morrisville, Vt., for several terms. He taught school in several places until the spring of 1851, when he came to Chicago and engaged in a dry goods store. The following winter he moved to Crete, Will County, Illinois, and taught school there, and also at Metamora, Woodford County. In 1864 he returned to Chicago and has been here ever since, engaged principally in the insurance business.

In 1852 Mr. Wood married Miss Nancy A. Morse of Hyde Park, Vt., a daughter of Dr. Morse; she died in 1858 and Mr. Wood married Miss Mary H. Walpole, of Keeseville, New York. Mr. Wood had six children, four of whom are now living.

(330)

GEORGE WILLIAM WOOD,

Of the Firm of W. G. Wood & Son, Local Agents.

George William Wood was born at Hyde Park, Vermont, July 9th, 1853. He received his education in the public schools of Chicago, and entered the insurance business at the same place in 1872.

Deceased Underwriters.

WILLIAM ASHWORTH,

Late General Agent British America Assurance Company.

Captain William Ashworth was born at Halifax, England; came to the United States in his youth. After nearly three years' service in the late war he entered the Insurance business at Rockford, Illinois, and subsequently was Special Agent for the Phenix of Brooklyn and aided in adjusting the losses resulting from the fire of October 9th, 1871. Previous to his appointment in the British America, he had been several years in the field for the Royal of England, in Mr. Chas. H. Case's department.

Mr. Ashworth's death took place July 6th, 1882.

JAMES AYARS,

Late of the Firm of Ayars & Magill. Local Agents.

Captain James Ayars was born in New Jersey fifty-seven years ago, practiced law in Covington, Ky., and removed to this city after the close of the war. He was one of our original Board of Fire Commissioners, and subsequently identified himself with the Internal Revenue office. When the Phoenix of Hartford established its Western Department, Capt. Ayars was appointed its Chicago Agent. For several years after the great fire of '71 he represented the Company in Milwaukee, but returned with it to this city, and for some time represented the Company with his nephew, as a member of the firm of Ayars & Magill.

Mr. Ayars was a man of generous impulses, kindly disposition, inflexible in adhering to what he believed to be right, and without resentment towards those with whom he differed. He could forgive and forget as readily as any one.

(335)

OSCAR W. BARRETT,

Late of the Firm of O. W. Barrett & Co., Local Agents.

Mr. Barrett was born in Bristol, N. Y., June 13th, 1836, removed to Rochester, then to New York and then to Chicago. In 1858 he entered the Insurance business, commencing with the Union of Chicago. Later he entered the office of B. W. Phillips as a clerk, becoming a partner in 1867. This old firm became that of O. W. Barrett & Co., for years one of the first Agencies in Chicago. The deceased was a member and trustee of the Second Baptist Church, a Knight Templar, a member of several clubs, prominent in the C. F. U. A. and the Fire Insurance Patrol, and Secretary of the Insurance Auxiliary Committee of the Columbian Exposition. Died July 2d, 1893.

AMASA S. BARRY,

Late General Adjuster.

Amasa S. Barry was born at Boston, Mass., on the 21st of March, 1821. He was educated in the public schools of Boston and entered business in 1840, as a druggist. In 1868 he became connected with the Insurance business and was made Treasurer and General Adjuster of the Old Illinois Mutual Insurance Company of Alton, Illinois. After the great Chicago fire of October, 1871, he entered the ranks of Independent Adjusters and was one of the first to make headquarters at Chicago.

Mr. Barry's experience in Insurance, while long and varied, was peculiarly directed in the channels of adjusting, in which department his record is marked with great ability, rare tact and signal success.

In 1844 he married Miss Catherine Riley. They had five children. He was Grand Treasurer of the I. O. O. F. of the State of Illinois for over twenty years, declining re-election on account of failing health, in 1881.

Mr. Barry died at Godfrey, Illinois, on the 17th of December, 1882, in the sixty-second year of his age.

JONATHAN J. BERNE,

Late General Adjuster of the Traders' Insurance Company.

Jonathan J. Berne was born near St. John, New Brunswick, about fifty-eight years ago, where his boyhood and early youth were spent and where the rudiments of his education were received. In early youth he came to the States, where he received a thorough business education. He chose the Insurance business for his calling and had his first experience with the Phoenix of Hartford, in the Western Department, with headquarters at Cincinnati, with which he remained as an Adjuster for some years, when he became associated with the well known J. B. Bennett, at Cincinnati, then the General Agent for the Aetna Fire. He acted in the capacity of Field Adjuster for the Aetna in the West until the formation by Mr. Bennett of the famous trio of Cincinnati Companies, the Andes, the Amazon and the Triumph. He then transferred his allegiance to these Companies, occupying the position of General Adjuster, and as such adjusted the losses sustained by the great Chicago fire and, later, those of the big Boston fire.

Upon the failure of these Companies he came to Chicago, about 1874, and for some time did general adjusting, but in 1876 abandoned it for a career on the Board of Trade. Here he remained until 1882, when he accepted the position of General Adjuster for the Traders' Insurance Company, where he remained continuously until his death. Mr. Berne spent much time writing on subjects connected with Underwriting, and his contributions were widely read and much appreciated. Among his works may be mentioned "Berne's Adjuster's Field Companion," published by the Argus, and received as authority everywhere. He was prominent in the work of the Fire Underwriters' Association of the Northwest, to which he contributed some of its most valued papers at its annual gatherings. He died in Jacksonville, Florida, February 25th, 1895.

GEORGE F. BISSELL,

Late General Agent of the Western Department of the Hartford Fire Insurance Company.

George F. Bissell was born at Manchester, Conn., in 1827. Engaged in the mercantile business at Springfield, Mass., and then at Dubuque, Iowa. Became Local Agent at Dubuque of the Hartford Fire Insurance Company, later its Special Agent for Iowa, and removed to Chicago in 1861. Appointed Manager of the extensive Western Department of the great Company May 1st, 1863, having been continuously in its service for over forty years. He was the dean of Western Fire Insurance and one of the first Underwriters of his time.

Mr. Bissell died at Asheville, N. C., June 25th, and was buried at Chicago June 28th, 1895. To all he was straightforward and plain spoken, a great Underwriter, an influential citizen, a wise counselor, a just judge, and an honest man.

THOMAS ROSS BURCH,

Late General Agent Western and Southern Department Phenix Insurance Company of New York.

Thomas Ross Burch was born in 1847 at Brooklyn, N.Y. His father, who is still living, is a clergyman. Thomas received his education in the schools of Brooklyn and Hartford, Conn., also under the private tutorship of his father. At the age of sixteen he entered the office of the Phenix as clerk in a minor position. He was advanced in the various clerkships as he demonstrated his capacity to fill them until he was promoted to the place of Assistant under the late William H. Van Voorhis, who for many years was the company's General Agent and Adjuster. On the death of Mr. Van Voorhis, Mr. Burch succeeded him, and remained there until early in 1874, when he came to Chicago as Manager of the Western Department. When he took charge of the Western business of the Company the annual premium receipts amounted to a little over $400,000 and during the thirteen years he managed it steadily increased the receipts until they had grown to over $2,500,000. This did not include the so-called "jumbo" or the inland marine premiums, but only the mercantile, dwelling and farm risks. This is a larger business than was done by any other company. Died June 12th, 1892.

HARVEY BUSH,

Late General Adjuster Fire Association of Philadelphia.

Harvey Bush was born near Oswego, New York, on the 9th day of December, 1823. He was still a youth when he came, with his parents, to Michigan, then a Territory, and settled upon a farm near Kalamazoo. He learned the wagon-maker's trade, and for ten years was Superintendent of that branch of mechanical labor in Jackson State prison. It was during this time that he acquired that intimate knowledge of machinery that was so valuable to him in adjusting fire losses.

He was married to Miss Laura M. Burdick, January 1st, 1847, and in 1854 moved with his family to Jackson.

In 1866 he was placed in nomination by the Republican party for Register of Deeds of Jackson County, and was elected to that office for two years, and re-elected for a third term. So faithful were his services that he eventually became a political power, not only in the community in which he lived, but throughout the State, and was sent as a delegate to the convention at Philadelphia that nominated Gen. Grant for President in 1872, and was active in that canvass against Greeley. So well did he represent the cause that he earned the warm friendship of "Zach." Chandler, whose political and personal favor he enjoyed during the lifetime of the great Republican chieftain.

In 1876 Mr. Bush consented to connect the business of Fire Insurance with that of his office of Register of Deeds, and took the supervision of the State of Michigan for the Security Insurance Company of New York, and later was connected with the American Fire Insurance Company of Philadelphia and the Fire Association of Philadelphia. His death occurred December 4th, 1883.

WILLIAM WALLACE CALDWELL,

Late General Adjuster Western Department American Fire Insurance Company of New York.

William Wallace Caldwell was born at Louisville, Ky., August 3d, 1835. His early life was spent among the Hoosiers, and when fifteen years old he began to "paddle his own canoe." He was clerk on a steamboat three years and then worked in his father's drug store at Jeffersonville, Ind., studying medicine at the same time. Upon reaching his majority he was appointed Postmaster at that place by President Buchanan, and there read law between the mails.

After the news from Sumter came Col. Caldwell was not long inactive. He organized the first company from Clark County, Ind., and was mustered into service as Captain of Co. B., Twenty-third Regiment Indiana Volunteers, in June, 1861, being then only twenty-six years old. He was with Commodore Foote on the gunboat that stormed Fort Henry, when nearly one-third of Caldwell's men then on duty went down. Upon the surrender he was assigned to the command that garrisoned the fort. After the battle of Shiloh he was deputized to raise a regiment at New Albany, Ind., and was next (in July, '62) made Colonel of the Eighty-first Regiment Indiana Volunteers. In August of that year he commanded Burbridge's Brigade in Major General Nelson's command, and later was assigned to the command of the Second Brigade, First Division, Twentieth Corps, Army of the Cumberland, and participated in the campaigns and battles of that army until July, '63, when he, upon being relieved by Brigadier General Carlin, resumed command of his regiment. Major General Rosecrans, in a letter to the President, said of Col. Caldwell: "He has more than once offered his life to his country and government."

In the year 1865, and while practicing law at Jeffersonville, Ind., he entered the Fire Insurance business. Three years later he was removed to Indianapolis, and came to Chicago in 1877, where he has held the position of General Agent or Manager for several companies. He was with the Peoples of Newark, N. J., then with the New Hampshire Fire, and next, for four years, with the New Orleans Insurance Company, and for three years was General Agent for the Factors and Traders. Col. Caldwell prepared and copyrighted several insurance blanks which were well received.

JOHN CAMERON,

John Cameron was born in Glasgow, Scotland, December 25th, 1832. His education was obtained in the schools and university of his native city. His early business enterprises were in manufacturing woolen goods under the direction of his father. He was married in Scotland but, resolving to try his fortune in America, came to Chicago in November, 1863, with his wife and two children. His first two years in this country were spent in learning the Packing business, which he then abandoned for Banking, and that, in turn, for Fire Insurance. His first connection in this, his future occupation, was with the Liverpool & London & Globe. The duties of his position were mostly clerical, and yet at the time of the great fire of 1871 he displayed such aptitude for his calling that he attracted the attention of the managers of the Northwestern National, and in 1875 was made Cook County Manager for that Company, a position which he held until his death, which occurred October 21st, 1895.

Mr. Cameron was a member of the Kenwood and Hyde Park Clubs, and for many years a trustee of the Hyde Park Presbyterian Church.

An experienced and conservative Underwriter, Mr. Cameron's loss is the removal of a well-known milestone from the street.

W. GUS. CHITTENDEN,

Late Manager of the Western Department of the Merchants' Insurance Company of New Jersey.

W. Gus. Chittenden was born at Greene, Chenango County, N. Y., March 4th, 1842. He was the youngest of four boys, of which only two are now living, Dr. Joseph H. Chittenden, of Binghamton, and Dr. Daniel J. Chittenden, of Addison. When he was quite young his family moved to Whitney's Point, N. Y., where he attended the village school, which was the best of that time. In August, 1862, he enlisted in Company D, One Hundred and Ninth New York Volunteers, as sergeant, and soon was promoted to first lieutenant. At the battle of Spottsylvania Court House he was seriously injured by the bursting of a shell, which was ultimately the cause of his death. After his return from the war he had a photograph gallery, which he was engaged in until the year of 1868, when he went to Binghamton and entered the Insurance business with Homer B. Boss. In 1882 he went on the road as Special Agent and Adjuster for the Merchants of Newark, N. J. In 1883 he was made General Manager of said Company with headquarters at Chicago, which position he held until the time of his death. In politics Mr. Chittenden was a Democrat, honored and respected by both parties. In 1867 he was nominated and elected Alderman of the Fourth Ward. He was a member of the Iroquois Club of Chicago and went with them to Washington to the first inauguration of President Cleveland.

Mr. Chittenden was married October 13th, 1870, to Miss Josephine M. Cusdy of Binghamton, N. Y.

He was a man of the highest character and strictest integrity, who had but one rule of conduct, first to know what was right, and then to do it. He passed away July 8th 1886, after a painful illness.

(344)

GEORGE C. CLARK,

Late of the Firm of George G. Clark & Co.

George C. Clarke died at Thomasville, Ga., April 5th, 1887. During the last few years of his life his failing health required his absence much of the time in a milder climate, but for over twenty years he was an active, prominent Underwriter in this city, representing a number of excellent companies in both a local and general capacity. He was also prominent in social and commercial circles in the Northwest, and enjoyed a large and influential acquaintance among those engaged in other than his chosen profession.

For over nine years, and until his health failed, he was an active and enthusiastic member of the N. W. Association, and much of the work during that period bears his imprint and inspiration. A genial companion, a true and faithful friend, a consistent and conscientious Christian gentleman, as well as an able and successful Underwriter, the memory of his excellent traits of character will ever be cherished by all who knew him.

WILLIAM BURGESS CORNELL,

Late Superintendent Western Department North British and Mercantile
Insurance Company.

William Burgess Cornell was born at Coventry, Chenango County, New York, December 11th, 1837. He was of English descent, both his grandfathers coming from England. His father, Dr. Edward Cornell, died when young Cornell was but twelve years of age, and he went to Addison, N. Y., where he entered the Academy, living with his brother, F. R. E. Cornell, then practicing law at Addison. After getting such an education as the Academy afforded, he entered a store in Addison as bookkeeper. In 1855 he and his brother came West to Minneapolis. Mr. Cornell was appointed Postmaster of Minneapolis and then studied law in his brother's office and in 1863 was admitted to the bar. Two years before that date he had married Miss Henrietta Wolford. While practicing law he became Agent for the Hartford and Phoenix Insurance Companies, and later was offered a position as correspondent in the Chicago General office.

Mr. Cornell continued in the service of the Hartford until 1869. From that date until 1872 he was employed by the Aetna Insurance Company as Special Agent for Kentucky and Tennessee. Later, in 1872, he was given the position of Manager of the North British and Mercantile Insurance Company for several States, with headquarters at Cincinnati, and in 1875 he returned to Chicago to take an enlarged jurisdiction as Superintendent of that Company's interests in connection with the late Walter E. Lewis. In 1879 Mr. Cornell became sole Manager, and remained so until the time of his death, which occurred October 3d, 1887.

Mr. Cornell could not be otherwise than prominent as an Underwriter. He was well known throughout the West and South. He frequently attended the meetings of the State Boards, where he was always welcome, and in 1882 he became President of the Fire Underwriters' Association of the Northwest. In his correspondence he was forcible, vivacious and witty, but, above all things, right to the point, and when occasion required him to rebuke wrong, his pen became a sledge hammer before which few could stand.

WILLIAM DAWSON CROOKE,

Late Manager Western Department Northern Assurance Company of England.

Major Crooke was born at Hebden Bridge, Yorkshire, England. His parents were members of the Baptist Church, and his father, the Rev. John Crooke, was minister of the church at that place. He came to this country in 1853, when about sixteen years of age, and settled near McGregor, Iowa, where he worked upon a farm for about two years. Later he studied law with Odell & Updegraff, at McGregor, Iowa, and was admitted to the bar in 1862.

During the Civil War he entered the United States service as Captain of Company B, Twenty-first Regiment Iowa Volunteer Infantry, August 18th, 1862, and was promoted to Major, January 25th, 1865. At the close of the war he returned to McGregor and was elected County Recorder of Deeds, and later became interested in the Insurance business.

He came to Chicago in 1876 and was appointed Assistant Manager of the Northwestern Department of the Royal Insurance Company of England, in which position he remained until 1882, when he was made Manager of the Western Department of the Northern Assurance Company of England, the duties of which he continued to discharge with satisfaction until the day of his death, which occurred on Friday, April 27th, 1894.

Major Crooke was married at McGregor, Iowa, in 1866, to Miss Sarah S. Updegraff, who survives him.

CHARLES CARROLL DANA,

Late General Adjuster Hartford Fire Insurance Company.

Charles Carroll Dana was born in Madison County, New York, December 3d, 1833; he was one of the six sons of Judge Sardis Dana, a man distinguished in business and political circles in the community in which he lived. In 1856, at the age of twenty-three, Mr. Dana removed to Oregon, Ills., and subsequently to the village of Lane, now called Rochelle, where he entered the drug business. He was married to Miss Anna R. Lovejoy, July 29th, 1858.

Mr. Dana was a Local Agent in 1863, and from that time until his death was engaged exclusively in the Insurance profession.

After a short but severe illness he died in Chicago, December 3d, 1881, leaving a wife and two children to mourn his loss.

THOMAS L. DEAN,

Late General Adjuster Hartford Fire Insurance Company.

Thomas L. Dean was born in Wayne County, New York, in 1840, and in his early boyhood moved to Allegan, Michigan. Here, at the age of eighteen, he engaged in the hardware business with J. B. Follette. He also served his country as a soldier in the War of the Rebellion, enlisting in the Third Michigan Cavalry; was appointed sergeant of his company, and in October, 1862, was commissioned second lieutenant, and first lieutenant in February, 1863, and captain in October, 1864.

After the close of the war he returned to Allegan, and soon after married Miss Mary Follette, daughter of his former employer. In 1869 he removed to Paw Paw and received an appointment in the Internal Revenue office. In 1872 he again returned to Allegan, where he engaged in the Insurance business, associating himself with A. E. Calkins. Later he was appointed Adjuster for the Manhattan Fire Insurance Company of New York, with headquarters at Indianapolis, Indiana. When that Company retired from business, Mr. Dean was appointed General Adjuster of the Hartford Fire Insurance Company, locating in Chicago. This position he filled with honor until the time of his death, which occurred December 17th, 1891.

JAMES CYRUS DOLMAN,

**Late General Adjuster Western Department Commercial Union Assurance
Company of England.**

James Cyrus Dolman was born in 1848 and died in Chicago, April 12th, 1882. He started in business at St. Joseph, Mo., with a prominent Agency in that city. In 1870 he moved to Cincinnati, entering the office of the Andes and Triumph Insurance Companies. He subsequently acted as Special Agent for the Andes, and at the time of his death had been connected nearly six years with the Commercial Union.

FREDERICK PITKIN FISHER,

Late of the Firm of Fisher Brothers.

Frederic P. Fisher was born at Oswego, New York, May 18th, 1828, and came of a New England family. After spending three years in France, from 1839 to 1842, with his father's family, studying in French schools most of the time, he was fitted for college at Williston Seminary, Easthampton, Mass., and graduated from Harvard University in 1848. In 1849 he entered the office of the Northwestern Insurance Company, at Oswego, New York, of which his father, George Fisher, was president. He came to Chicago in 1850 and was appointed Local Agent of the Northwestern Fire and Marine Insurance Company. He afterwards engaged in the timber business, from 1854 to 1857, under the firm name of Price & Fisher. He then entered the Insurance business again, as Cashier for L. D. Olmstead & Co., Real Estate and Insurance. He was an active Republican, and during the Rebellion warmly supported the Government. In 1865 he formed a partnership with Edward M. Teall, in the Fire Insurance business, which was dissolved in 1875. He then entered into partnership with his twin brother, Francis P. Fisher, under the name of Fisher Brothers, in which firm he remained until his death, which occurred August 28th, 1886. He was a good citizen, a true friend, of a high sense of honor, and faithful to every trust reposed in him. He was an accomplished Underwriter and jealous of the interests of his clients and of the companies he represented.

Mr. Fisher was a prominent member of the First Unitarian Society from the time of his arrival in Chicago, in 1850, to the time of his death, in 1886. He was a member of the Harvard and Calumet Clubs and very active in the French Club, and was treasurer of his church for many years.

JAMES BOVARD FLOYD,

Late Local Agent.

James Bovard Floyd was born in Butler County, Pennsylvania, May 14th, 1842, and died October 17th, 1881. When he was about nine years of age his family moved to Chicago and he attended Gleason's School for Boys, finishing his education in Pennsylvania. When he was fourteen years of age his father died and he accepted a position in a dry goods house in Philadelphia, boarding with two Quaker ladies who became his lifelong friends. He came back to Chicago before he was twenty-one years old and entered the Insurance office of T. L. Miller. In 1870 he became Chicago manager of the Underwriters' Agency of New York, which position he held during the great fire and until 1875, when he was offered and accepted the Agency of the Phenix of Brooklyn and the Fire men's of Dayton, Ohio, with which he was connected at the time of his death. He was awarded a gold medal by the Chicago Underwriters' Association for his integrity in the adjustment of losses during the Chicago fire.

Mr. Floyd was married at Chicago, Ills., on the 24th of June, 1868, to Miss Ruth Wing and had three children.

SIRENO FRENCH.

Sireno French was born August 12th, 1810, at Otisco, N. Y., and after reaching man's estate he became interested in the Insurance business and the interest remained with him until he died. He was a man of strong intellectual gifts and an enthusiastic and energetic nature, that made him successful in most of his undertakings. Thus he became a successful Insurance man, and in later years a successful writer.

In the early '60's he came to Chicago as the General Agent of the City Fire of Hartford, and upon the organization of the Orient, in 1867, was made General Agent of that Company. He was an earnest student of underwriting, and mastered its minutest details, and when Mr. B. W. French, his son, was ready for active business life, took him into the Agency and trained him to successfully fill the position of General Agent for the old Company. During these years of active managerial work Mr. French was constantly writing and talking on Insurance subjects, and he was always interesting. He was also a pleasant and genial man and had many warm friends—there are many of them on the street in this city to-day—who admired him for his earnestness and honesty, as well as his unusual intellectual endowments.

Ten years or more ago he gave the General Agency business into the hands of his son, Mr. B. W. French, and returned to New York State to live in retirement. He built him a pleasant home on the banks of Lake Conesus, and called it "Castle Content." But he soon found something lacking about the castle. It was not all to him that the name implied, and casting about for the lacking ingredient he concluded it was the absence of the Insurance business, with which he had been so long identified. So he arranged with the National of Hartford to establish a Local Agency at Conesus, and though he wrote but few policies each year, he was satisfied. He kept abreast of the times, and wrote a great deal on the subject of Geology and Insurance.

His last article for publication was on the subject of Stock and Mutual Insurance. The article was a concise exposition of the weakness of Mutual Insurance, and was decidedly interesting.

Mr. French was married at Richmond, Ontario County, New York, in 1835, to Miss Jane E. Whitney. He was eighty-one years of age at the time of his death, and his long life had been an honorable and useful one.

JONATHAN GOODWIN, JR.

Late of the Firm of Goodwin & Pasco.

Jonathan Goodwin, Jr., was born in Hartford, Conn., March 11th, 1840. During his boyhood Mr. Goodwin attended the public schools of Hartford, and afterward the high school. He very early showed those sterling traits of character which marked his maturer years. After passing through the high school course in a praiseworthy manner he entered immediately into business, learning the ins and outs in the old fashion, namely, by an apprenticeship in the hardware establishment of Terry & Lester, until he was twenty-one years of age. He then entered the office of the Aetna Insurance Company of Hartford as cashier. Mr. Goodwin, at the end of two years, feeling there was a wider field of effort for which he was qualified, moved to Chicago in the fall of 1865. He soon after entered into partnership with Mr. Chas. H. Hunt, formerly of the firm of Hubbard & Hunt. This partnership, under the name of Hunt & Goodwin, continued until June, 1870, when it was brought to a close by the death of Mr. Hunt.

After Mr. Hunt's decease, Mr. C. H. Pasco was admitted into partnership. Mr. Pasco was an early friend of Mr. Goodwin's, and a man of excellent qualities and fine business talents. The firm name was Goodwin & Pasco, representing the Aetna and other companies.

Mr. Goodwin was a member of the Second Presbyterian Church. He was a man of agreeable presence, hopeful and ardent, but never indiscreet; fond of home life, and not caring to shine in the political world. He was married to Miss Ripley, daughter of Mr. Edwin G. Ripley, at one time Second Vice-President of the Aetna Insurance Company, at Hartford, Conn. They had two daughters, Helen Ripley and Mary Jeannette.

GEORGE D. GOULD,

Late Independent Adjuster.

George D. Gould was born at Hanover, N. H., on the 26th of March, 1836. He was educated in the common schools and lived on a farm until 1854, when he engaged as clerk in a dry goods store at Bradford, Vermont. He came West in 1856 and worked in a grocery store until 1857, and then two years in the Chicago Post Office. In 1859 he went across country to California, coming back in 1860 and engaging as clerk in a grocery store in Cambridge, Illinois, until 1865, when he entered the Insurance business at Moline, Illinois, as Local Agent, afterward accepting the position of State Agent of New York Underwriters' Agency.

Mr. Gould was a member of the Masonic Order, up to thirty-second degree, and was Master of "Doric Lodge."

JOSEPH S HARRIS,

Late General Agent Metropole Fire Insurance Company of France.

Joseph S. Harris was born in Rochester, New York, and was of Holland-Scotch descent. Commencing local Insurance practice at Cleveland, Tenn., in 1867, he shortly after began field work, serving with various companies. The Underwriters' Agency of New York, the Andes Insurance Company, the Cleveland Fire Insurance Company, the Franklin Insurance Company of Philadelphia, and the Insurance Company of North America, until, in April, 1874, he became Associate Manager for the Northwest of the Niagara Insurance Company of New York, remaining in that position until 1879, when he accepted the General Agency of the Metropole Fire Insurance Company for the Western States, which position he held at the time of his death, which occurred in Cincinnati, Ohio, December 15th, 1881.

FRANK B. HOSMER,

Late of the Firm of D. S. Munger & Co.

Frank B. Hosmer was born at Concord, Mass., February 23d, 1849, but removed with his parents to Boston at an early age. July 25th, when not yet sixteen years old, he graduated from the Brimmer school with the highest honors, taking the Franklin medal. He removed to Chicago in 1870, associating himself with his brothers, R. W. and J. W. Hosmer, in the Fire Insurance business, the firm being R. W. Hosmer & Co. Ten years later he became a member of the firm of D. S. Munger & Co., with which firm he remained until his death.

In January, 1876, he married Emma, eldest daughter of the Rev. Robert Collyer, who with three sons survive him.

Mr. Hosmer died at Chicago, Illinois, August 8th, 1890.

W. I. HOWARD,

Late Special Agent Western Assurance Company of Toronto.

W. I. Howard was born at Batavia, New York, in the year 1837, and died at Cincinnati, Ohio, February 5th, 1894. His earlier years up to 1871 were passed as a clerk in various mercantile establishments.

While in the employ of the firm of McLean & Sons, lumber manufacturers, at Saginaw, Michigan, he accepted the Agency of several Insurance Companies, and from that time until his death was steadily engaged in the business, either as Local Agent or in the field. He was for many years a member of the Fire Underwriters' Association of the Northwest, and always enthusiastic over its work.

GURDON S. HUBBARD,

First Chicago Agent Aetna Insurance Company.

Gurdon S. Hubbard was born in Vermont, in 1802, and came to Chicago in 1818, when it was only a small trading post. From this early date he had been prominently identified with the history and growth of Chicago. His experience at first was that of a fur trader, then that of a merchant, then as a large real estate owner and speculator. At different times in the early history of Chicago, owing to his intimate knowledge of the country and his intelligence in business and political matters, he had been consulted by government officials and leading men. At the time of the great fire he had letters from Webster, Clay and others, which were treasured as souvenirs of the past and were highly prized on account of the writers, but which were lost, together with many other valuable relics of early times.

Mr. Hubbard was the first Agent of the Aetna Insurance Company, being appointed to fill that post in 1831, and in that year issued the first policy of Insurance issued in Chicago or Cook County. This first policy was on exhibition in the Historical Library of Chicago until destroyed in the fire of 1871.

For over thirty years Mr. Hubbard continued to represent the Aetna in Chicago, first as G. S. Hubbard, then as Hubbard & Hunt, until 1867, when Mr. Hubbard retired from the business and Hunt & Goodwin became the Agents. During the entire term of his Agency he enjoyed the most implicit confidence of this company, and upon the business done by him through his long period of service it realized a handsome profit. Besides the Aetna, he represented several other leading companies, among them being the Phoenix of Hartford, of which he was also the first representative, and which he retained for many years.

CHARLES HUNT,

Late of the Firm of Hunt & Goodwin, Local Agents.

Charles H. Hunt was born in Rochester, N. Y., in 1830. His father, Solomon Hunt, was a native of Stafford, Vermont, and an uncle of the present United States Senator, Justin S. Morrill.

At the early age of fourteen Mr. Hunt came to Chicago to visit his cousin, James Rochester, then a leading commission merchant of Chicago, and entered his employ. Within a year Mr. Rochester's health failed and he was compelled to return East. Gurdon S. Hubbard, then a prominent packer and insurance agent, was attracted by the boy's intelligence and gave him employment in the office of the Aetna Fire Insurance Company of Hartford, Conn. Here Mr. Hunt served with marked fidelity until in 1848 he was made bookkeeper. In this capacity his ability soon won the confidence of his employers, and he was made a special partner in the insurance business, receiving one-fourth of the profits.

This arrangement continued until 1858, when he was given an equal interest in both the packing and insurance business, the former of which had grown into considerable magnitude. The firms were then G. S. Hubbard & Co. and Hubbard & Hunt, the latter style of firm being adopted for the insurance branch of their interests. In 1867 Mr. Hunt retired from the packing business and purchased Mr. Hubbard's interest in the insurance agency. Mr. Hunt sold a one-half interest in the insurance business to Jonathan Goodwin, Jr., and from that time the firm of Hunt & Goodwin was one of the leading fire insurance agencies of the city, representing the Security of New York, the Rogers Williams of Providence and a number of other companies. The Aetna was also represented by the firm until Mr. Hunt's death, June 9th, 1870.

Upon the organization of the Citizens' Fire Brigade of Chicago, Ill., November 19th, 1858, Mr. Hunt was selected Chairman of the Firemen's Committee.

In 1860 Mr. Hunt was married to Miss Eleonora Shaw of Madison, Ind. They had two daughters, Jennie C., who died February, 1875, and Lizzie Shaw, born September 21st, 1862.

EDWARD L. IRETON,

Late General Adjuster.

Edward L. Ireton was for twenty years General Adjuster for the Western Department of the Phoenix Insurance Company of Hartford, and afterward General Agent at Cincinnati of the Central Department of the California Insurance Company. For several years he had been an independent Adjuster in Chicago, doing such work as he could find to do, and, though laboring under physical infirmities, holding on manfully to the end. Mr. Ireton was a native of Ireland and only fifty-four years old at the time of his death, which occurred May 21st, 1893.

THOMAS W. JOHNSTON,

Colonel Thos. W. Johnston had a fine war record. He was made Colonel of the Second Michigan Cavalry in 1864. He joined the Western Department of the Agricultural Insurance Company, in 1872, as Special Agent and Adjuster, serving as such until the Sun of London came here, when he was appointed Western General Agent for said Company, which position he filled until the time of his death, which occurred in 1883, at his old home at Marshall, Michigan.

Colonel Johnston had an excellent Insurance record, and was honored and respected by all in the profession.

GUSTAVUS H. KOCH.

Gustavus H. Koch was born at Geissen, Germany, in August, 1832, and was educated in Heidelburg. Colonel Koch came to this country about 1859, and after residing for a while in St. Louis, Mo., moved to St. Joseph, where he engaged in the grocery business with Henry Bourgesser. When the war broke out he entered the army of his adopted country, and retired at the close of same with the rank of Colonel. Soon after the close of the war he formed the wholesale grocery firm of Koch, Chew & Co., which business he conducted successfully for a number of years. While a member of this firm he was elected treasurer of Buchanan County, Missouri. In the year 1873 he was selected by President Grant to represent the State of Missouri as Commissioner at the Vienna Exposition. In 1875 the firm of Koch, Chew & Co. retired from business and Colonel Koch became president of the German Savings Bank of St. Joseph, and the same year, in connection with banking business, he became Agent at St. Joseph of several leading Fire Insurance Companies, for which he did a satisfactory business.

In June, 1876, he removed with his family to St. Louis and formed a partnership with William R. Kerr, under the firm name of Koch & Kerr, for the transaction of a Local Fire Insurance business. This firm was dissolved in 1878 and Colonel Koch became General Agent for the West of the Hamburg-Magdeburg Insurance Company, with headquarters at St. Louis. In November, 1879, after having successfully planted the company throughout the West, he came to realize the necessity of having his headquarters in the Insurance center of the West, and moved his department to Chicago. He continued his representation of the Hamburg-Magdeburg until May, 1882, when the company ceased business in this country and honorably discharged all its obligations. After the retirement of this company he continued in the Local Fire Insurance business and added thereto the Steamship business and the General Agency of the Fidelity & Casualty Company of New York, in which business he continued until his death, which occurred at New Brighton, Staten Island, on the 29th of May, 1886.

WALTER E. LEWIS,

Late Adjuster of Fire Losses.

Walter E. Lewis died at Hinsdale, Illinois, November 21st, 1886, aged forty-six years. He entered the Hartford Insurance Company in 1865, and was afterward General Adjuster for the Western Department for two years. Thereupon Mr. Lewis became an independent Adjuster and in that position death found him.

As an Adjuster of Fire Losses he had no superior. In the realm of figures he was a king. To quote from the "In Memoriam" resolved on by the Fire Underwriters' Association of the Northwest, he was "a man of commanding ability in his profession, of unswerving integrity in its prosecution, and uncompromising. fidelity to every trust reposed in him."

CASPAR E. MANTZ,

Late Assistant Manager Springfield Fire and Marine Insurance Company.

Caspar E. Mantz was born in Frederick City, Maryland, on the 19th of December, 1842, and was educated in the Catholic school of that city. Leaving school when ten years of age, he entered a small country store, and at the age of eleven was correcting proof in a printing office. Thence he was a bookkeeper in St. Louis, and came to Chicago in 1860 in the same capacity for Young Bros. & Co., entering the Insurance business about 1867 or 1868. He was a member of the Union League Club.

Mr. Mantz was a remarkable man, had a prodigious memory, and could remember facts, faces and dates of history. He knew French, Latin and German; was a constant student and a great reader.

He was mild and gentle; kind and loving to his mother, and in no way gave her any trouble or worry, and ever mindful of her in the smallest degree. He was tender hearted and loved his family devotedly; was charitable and always willing to help his friends.

JAMES ROSS MILLER,

Late of the Firm of Miller, Drew & Company.

James Ross Miller was born in Rochester, New York, and was a graduate of Michigan University and an admitted member of the legal profession. He commenced the business of Fire Underwriting with Chas. W. Drew, his late partner, which he pursued with an assiduity, industry and perseverance worthy of all praise; and by his gentlemanly bearing, his high social qualities and honorable dealing he secured the esteem and friendship of every member of the fraternity. He was a member of Grace Episcopal Church. His death occurred Monday, November 29th, 1880, when he was thirty-nine years old.

EUGENE S. MORSE,

Late of the Firm of Edwards, Morse & Klee.

Eugene S. Morse was born in Brunswick, Me., in 1866, and died July 21, 1895. Coming to Chicago in 1888, he entered the office of the Liverpool & London & Globe as a clerk; soon after he engaged with A. R. Edwards in the insurance business, and in 1893 became a member of the firm of Edwards, Morse & Klee

HENRY L. PASCO,

Late of the Firm of Goodwin & Pasco.

Major Henry L. Pasco was a native of East Hartford, Conn. At the commencement of Civil War he entered the service as Captain, taking part in several actions, suffering imprisonment for several months and returning as Major of his Regiment. In 1865 he entered the service of the Aetna Insurance Company as Special Agent, and in 1870 removed to Chicago, becoming associated with Mr. Goodwin in the well-known firm of Goodwin & Pasco, remaining until 1877 in the agency business, when he returned to Hartford, taking the position of Special Agent of the Aetna for New York and the Eastern States. He died suddenly June 3d, 1882, from an attack of jaundice, aged forty-two. During his residence in this city he had endeared himself to Local and General Agents, and when the sad news of his death was received a joint meeting of the Chicago Board of Underwriters and of the Underwriters' Exchange was held at which appropriate resolutions of respect and sympathy were reported.

OAKLEY B. PELLET,

Late of the Firm of Pellet & Hunter, General Agents.

Oakley B. Pellet was born December 14, 1834, in Sussex County, New Jersey. He engaged in mercantile business at Newton, N. J., for several years, and afterwards conducted a Local Insurance business in that town, retiring to become Special Agent of the Hudson Fire Insurance Company of Jersey City. He came to Chicago in 1873, to establish a western department of that company, and again became interested in Local business in connection with the General Agency. The firm of Pellet & Hunter was formed in 1884.

Mr. Pellet died January 14th, 1887. He had an extended experience, both as Local and General Agent, was an Underwriter of ability and a thorough business man. For his companies he did good service, and in the management of their business was skillful and popular.

(369)

EDMUND E. RYAN,

Late of the Firm of E. E. Ryan & Company, Local Agents.

Captain Edmund E. Ryan was born in Philadelphia in 1833, coming to Illinois and settling in Peoria about 1858. Shortly after the outbreak of the Civil War he enlisted in Company A of the Seventeenth Illinois Infantry. While serving in Missouri as a bearer of dispatches, he was captured and sentenced to be shot, but fortunately managed to escape. Soon after he was appointed Lieutenant, and while acting Captain of his company in Georgia was again taken prisoner and confined for several months in Andersonville Prison, where ill-cooked food impaired his digestion and laid the foundation of severe gastric trouble, ending in consumption. At the close of the war Captain Ryan was appointed Supervisor and Adjuster of the Illinois Mutual Insurance Company of Alton, Ills. Being also in the Local business he was with F. A. Hoffman in 1868, the firm name being changed to E. E. Ryan & Co., in 1870. Both for health and in the interests of his company he went to California, Texas, Colorado and New Mexico. For many years he resided in Hyde Park, taking an active interest in local matters, serving as a member of the Department of Trustees in 1874, also as a Water Commissioner, and he will always be remembered as a gentlemanly neighbor, and an active and faithful official. In his business relations his mental vigor, executive will, and generous heart combined to make him successful and respected, and this aided largely in giving a position in the agency field to the companies represented by him of inestimable value to his associates, now successors to the firm name. He died in Chicago on the 29th of January, 1883.

SIMEON SCHUPP.

Simeon Schupp was born in Germany in 1828. As a boy of fourteen he came to this country and grew up in the South, living at New Orleans for a number of years. He came West and first engaged in the Fire Insurance business at Naperville, Illinois, with the German Insurance Company of Freeport, Illinois, and with the exception of one year, in which he performed field work for the Milwaukee Mechanics Insurance Company, his lot was cast with the German.

In the year 1889 Mr. Schupp was appointed Manager for Chicago and Cook County for the Milwaukee Mechanics Insurance Company, and the German of Freeport, Illinois, both companies writing a joint policy for said territory. His long residence in Chicago gave him a thorough acquaintance with the field intrusted to his care, and aided by his experience, keen and discerning mind and his well-known conservatism he could not fail to be eminently successful.

Mr. Schupp died at Chicago on the 10th of December, 1893.

EDWIN ARTEMAS SIMONDS,

Late General Agent Western Department Greenwich Fire Insurance Company, New York.

Edwin Artemas Simonds was born in Boston, Mass., on December 4th, 1834. His father was cashier of the Mechanics' Bank, of Boston, for over fifty years.

Mr. Simonds received his education in the Boston schools, graduating from the High School, and afterwards was a student of Amherst College. Bidding adieu to student life, he became a clerk in the city of Boston, and next entered the employ of the Old Colony Railroad, where he remained in various capacities for about six years. He then became messenger for the Freeman's National Bank and worked through the various grades until he became Paying Teller. He resigned this position to accept the assistant cashiership in the City Treasurer's office, where he remained until the breaking out of the war. He first enlisted in the "thirty days' service," and then went into the navy, where he became a sailing master, and did some good service for the government. After the war. Mr. Simonds engaged in the Insurance business. He was marine adjuster with Gen. Thos. S. Tyler (deceased), of Boston, for two years. He then came West and joined the Western Department of the Insurance Company of North America, under Mr. J. F. Downing, where he remained in various capacities, the last being State Agent and Adjuster for Iowa. On the decease of Mr. J. S. Harris in 1880, he received the appointment of General Agent for the Western Department of the Metropole Insurance Company of France, and in 1881 was chosen in the same field for the City of London Fire Insurance Company. For ten years he was Secretary of the Union, and at the time of his death was General Agent of the Greenwich Insurance Company of New York, headquarters in Chicago.

On a fateful day in October, 1893, he closed his desk and said: "I go to the Hospital. My work is done. My deeds are recorded. If I do not return I bequeath to my successor a clean sheet." He never returned to his desk, dying under an operation on the 2d day of November, 1893.

Mr. Simonds was a member of the Masonic Order and other fraternal organizations; also the Union League Club.

AZEL W. SPAULDING,

Late Manager Western Department Home Mutual Insurance Company.

Azel W. Spaulding was born at Montpelier, Vermont, May 29th, 1837. In the spring of 1839 he, with his parents, removed to Kansas. Soon after the breaking out of the War of the Rebellion, May 29th, 1861, his twenty-third birthday, he enlisted as a private in Company E, First Regiment of Kansas Volunteers; the same day he was promoted to First Sergeant, and on the 5th of June to Second Lieutenant. He participated in numerous skirmishes, the memorable battle of Wilson's Creek being among them. Owing to failing health, caused by a sunstroke received on a long march in Missouri, he resigned October 31st, 1861, and returned to his home in Valley Falls, Jefferson County, Kansas. In 1862 he was elected State Senator from that county, he being the youngest member of that body. He entered the Insurance business in 1869 as Local Agent for the Phoenix of Hartford, at Atchison, Kansas. He continued in the Local business until 1874, securing the Agency of the Aetna, Franklin of Philadelphia, and other leading companies, until the time when he accepted a position with the Franklin Insurance Company of Philadelphia as General Adjuster for the Western States, and took up his residence at St. Louis, Mo. He continued with the Franklin until 1881, when he accepted the management of the Western Department of the Standard Insurance Company of London. He then became Manager of the Western Department of the Home Mutual Insurance Company of California, with which company he continued until his health failed him in December, 1884. He removed to Atchison, Kas., where he died in 1888, being 49 years of age.

THOMAS UNDERWOOD,

Late Independent Adjuster.

Thomas Underwood was born in Washington City, D. C., August 19th, 1829, and was a little over fifty-eight years of age at the time of his death. When sixteen years old he, with his parents, removed to Cambridge City, Indiana, where he was employed in a hardware store owned by his brother-in-law, the late Charles H. Raymond. Upon reaching his majority he was married at Batavia, New York, to Miss Ann Eliza Wilson. Soon after his marriage he came to La Fayette, where he embarked in the hardware business. In 1853, upon the organization of the city government, he was elected to represent the Third Ward in the City Council. He was also the first chief of the Fire Department. He equipped and ran at his own expense a hand engine for putting out fires. The horse he called General U. S. Grant, the engine was named Schuyler Colfax, and the darky boy driver was called Horace Greeley. He made it interesting for the City Department, as he always aimed to reach a fire first. In 1862 he joined the Twenty-second Indiana Regiment, and was commissioned Quartermaster. At the close of the war he returned to La Fayette, Indiana, and took a position with Peckham & Smith in the Real Estate and Insurance business, afterwards becoming their partner, and finally succeeding them in the business. In 1871 his son, Charles R. Underwood, became a member of the firm, which has since been known as T. Underwood & Son. Since 1881, Mr. Underwood has spent most of his time in Chicago. Seven years ago he accepted an important position with the Home Insurance Company of New York, with headquarters at Chicago. Besides these varied business pursuits he was very prominent in secret societies. For nearly forty years he was a member of the La Fayette Lodge, No. 15, and Wabash Encampment, No. 6, I. O. O. F., Past Grand Master of the Grand Lodge of the State, and a member of the Supreme Lodge of the world. He was also a member of the Improved Order of Red Men, and several years ago joined the Masonic Fraternity, and was a member of the Uniformed Patriarchs and also of the Knights Templar. In all these societies he was a hard worker.

He died February 5, 1888.

SIDNEY P. WALKER,

[Late]Secretary Globe Insurance Company, Chicago.

Sidney P. Walker succeeded Mr. C. N. Holden as Secretary of the Fireman's in 1865, and made a brilliant record for himself and that company from that time until the great fire came and swept the company out of existence. Being a large stockholder of the company he was consequently a loser by that disaster. However, he did not lose his courage, for no sooner had the smoke cleared away than he formed a partnership with Mr. W. A. Lowell, and the firm of Walker & Lowell at once started as General and Local Agents of the Allemania of Cleveland. Subsequently two or three more companies were added to their list. In 1873 he was elected Secretary of the Globe Insurance Company and in that capacity he hoped to repeat the success that had made the Fireman's one of the leading companies in the country. This desire was not to be realized, for the second big fire (of July 14th, 1884,) came and the claims against the Globe footed up nearly $100,000, all of which were paid. From this time may be traced the commencement of the breaking up of Mr. Walker's health. Had disaster ceased for a time and allowed the company to recuperate all would no doubt have been well, but it was decreed otherwise, for the losses accumulated from month to month in such amounts as to cause Mr. Walker no little anxiety to know how to pay them when due. It was this anxiety and the consequent strain on his system that laid the foundation of the disease which he finally succumbed to on the 22d of January, 1884. As an employer he was one of the kindest and always looked after the interests of those under him. As a friend his friendship was strong. As an Underwriter he was one of the ablest in the profession.

DAVID B. WARNER,

Late General Agent, Western Department Phoenix Assurance Company of London, Eng.

David B. Warner was born in Dayton, Ohio, July 8th, 1833, and at the time of his decease was in his fifty-ninth year. In 1880 he came to Chicago as the General Western Agent of the Phoenix Assurance Company of London, England, which position he held until the time of his death. His Insurance experience was long, varied and successful. He was essentially a self-made man, having begun life as a farmer boy. By force of energy and uprightness of character, he forced his way from the bottom to the top of the ladder. As a business man his life was successful; as a citizen he was honored; as a husband and father he was beloved, and his death, which occurred on the 19th of March, 1892, was deeply regretted.

SAMUEL ROHRER WARNER

Late Assistant General Agent Phoenix Assurance Company of London, Eng.

Samuel Rohrer Warner was born near Dayton, Ohio, January 25th, 1863, of American parents. He was educated in the Common Schools of Dayton, and in the Business College of the same place. He commenced business as Bookkeeper in a Wholesale Grocery house in Dayton, Ohio, and from there went to the Phoenix of London, in Chicago, October, 1882. He was Assistant General Agent of the Phoenix of London, and was compelled to resign on account of ill health. He was married in Chicago, May 10th, 1888, to Miss Mary B. Rawleigh, of Chicago, and had one child—a son.

Mr. Warner was a member of the Ashland Club of Chicago. He died in Colorado in 1895.

WILLIAM WARREN,

Late Resident-Secretary Liverpool & London & Globe Insurance Company.

William Warren was born in the town of Uffington, County of Berks, England, on the 22d day of March, 1819. Coming to this country at an early period he was appointed Local Agent of the Liverpool & London & Globe Insurance Company in Cleveland, Ohio, in 1853, and from there he moved to Cincinnati in 1859 to fill the position of General Agent for the same company. He came to Chicago in 1860 and a still greater promotion was accepted by him in 1875, as Resident Secretary, and he took charge of the immense business of this company for all the Northwestern States and Territories, and for twelve years he so managed the affairs of the Liverpool & London & Globe Insurance Company in the Northwest that not only were profits made each year, but the company everywhere was made more popular.

A continual service in one company, the Liverpool & London & Globe, for thirty-five years, goes to show the fidelity to duty of Mr. Warren, and proves conclusively the high record in which he was held by the management of this grand organization. He was a gentleman of the old school, always polite and affable to those who had business with him. As an Underwriter, Mr. Warren had no superior in this part of the world, being cautious, conservative and eminently rigid in his notions, and of the highest probity, both in his profession and in private life. He died November 10th, 1889.

JAMES M. WHITEHEAD,

Late Special Agent and Adjuster Imperial Fire Insurance Company of London.

James Mordock Whitehead was born at Brampton, Canada, March 17th, 1850, and died after a brief illness at Chicago, Illinois, February 25th, 1890. His connection with the Insurance business dates from about the time of the Chicago fire of 1871, and extended to all the positions incident to the Local and General business, from clerk and policy writer in a Local office, to Adjuster, Special Agent and Manager in the general field. His business career brought him in contact and intercourse with almost the entire Underwriting fraternity of the Western and Northern States, and he was known as a careful, prudent and conservative underwriter, and an Adjuster whose aim was to do equal justice to all with whom his business brought him in contact.

The members of the Northwestern Association, to whom he was so long and favorably known, will ever treasure the memory of one who was endeared to them by acts of kindness and courtesy.

The funeral services were conducted under the auspices of Apollo Commandery, Knights Templar, of Chicago, of whom he was an honored member.

HENRY BROWN WILLMARTH,

Late Independent Adjuster.

Henry Brown Willmarth was born at South Adams, Mass., on the 14th of November, 1814, and was educated in the schools and academies of North and South Adams. He commenced his business life as clerk and assistant manager in his father's store. Leaving South Adams he went to New York and took a position as clerk with Stanton & Jarvis, wholesale grocers. Later he formed a partnership with Oliver B. Stanton and sold goods in Mexico during the Mexican War. After his return from Mexico he went into business with Col. H. C. Bowman, of New York City.

Mr. Willmarth came to Chicago in 1852 and entered the insurance business at that place in 1855.

On the 12th of September, 1849, Mr. Willmarth was married at Barrington, Cook County, Ill., to Miss Janet Brown, and had six sons and one daughter.

Owing to failing health Mr. Willmarth was obliged to resign his business and go to Denver, where he died on the 29th of July, 1887.

(380)

ALFRED WRIGHT.

Late Secretary Chicago Board of Fire Underwriters.